FHA Refinance Options Made Simple

Streamline, Rate-and-Term, and Cash-Out Refinancing Explained for Homeowners

By Joseph G. Correa

Licensed Mortgage Broker, Finibi Mortgage

Copyright & Legal Notice

Published by Live Stronger Faster

First Edition, 2026

Table of Contents

Foreword

For most homeowners, refinancing sounds simple on the surface. Lower your rate. Reduce your payment. Maybe pull out a little cash. Yet for millions of FHA borrowers, refinancing feels confusing, intimidating, and often risky—not because the options aren't powerful, but because they are poorly explained, misunderstood, or presented in ways that benefit lenders more than borrowers. This book exists to change that. FHA Refinance Options Made Simple was written for everyday homeowners who want clarity, confidence, and control over one of the most important financial tools they will ever use.

FHA loans are often introduced as "starter loans," but that label misses the bigger picture. The truth is that FHA loans are not just about getting into a home—they are about staying in the home, improving affordability over time, and using smart refinancing strategies to protect and strengthen your financial future. Refinancing is where many FHA borrowers either make their smartest move or their most expensive mistake. Understanding when to refinance, how each FHA refinance option works, and how to avoid common traps can mean the difference between building long-term stability or staying stuck in an endless cycle of fees, resets, and missed opportunities. This book is the seventh in The FHA

Homeownership & Wealth Series for a reason. By the time a borrower is considering refinancing, they are no longer a beginner. They have already navigated the homebuying process. They have lived with their mortgage. They have experienced interest rate changes, monthly payment pressures, and real-life financial decisions that don't always fit neatly into lender scripts or online calculators. Refinancing is not a theoretical concept—it's a real decision with real consequences. That is why this book focuses on practical understanding, not sales language.

One of the biggest problems in the mortgage industry is that refinancing is often marketed as an emotional decision instead of a strategic one. Homeowners are told to refinance because "rates dropped," because "everyone else is doing it," or because "you can skip a payment." Rarely are borrowers taught how to evaluate whether refinancing actually benefits them over the long term. Rarely are they shown how to compare a streamline refinance to a rate-and-term refinance or how to determine when a cash-out refinance helps—and when it quietly harms—their financial position. This book aims to give borrowers the tools to ask better questions before signing anything.

FHA refinancing is unique because it offers options that do not exist with most conventional loans. The FHA Streamline

Refinance, for example, is one of the most borrower-friendly refinance programs in the entire mortgage system—yet many homeowners do not understand how it works or when it should be used. At the same time, FHA cash-out refinancing can be a powerful way to access equity, but only when it is done with intention, discipline, and a clear plan. Used incorrectly, it can delay wealth-building and increase long-term costs. Used correctly, it can create flexibility, reduce high-interest debt, and open doors that were previously closed.

This book was written with a simple promise: no jargon without explanation, no pressure tactics, and no assumptions about what the borrower "should" do. Every homeowner's situation is different. Some borrowers refinance to lower their payment. Others refinance to shorten their loan term. Some need relief during financial transitions, while others want to position themselves for future investments or stability. FHA refinance programs are flexible by design, but flexibility only works when the borrower understands the rules of the game.

Another reason this book matters is timing. Many borrowers refinance at the wrong time—not because they lack intelligence, but because they lack information. They refinance too soon and pay unnecessary upfront mortgage insurance again. They refinance too late and miss out on savings that could have compounded over years. They refinance into a slightly lower rate without understanding how closing costs, loan term resets, and mortgage insurance interact behind the scenes. This book slows the process down so borrowers can see the full picture before making a decision that may affect them for decades.

Refinancing is also deeply emotional, even when it shouldn't be. A home represents safety, stability, and achievement. When financial stress enters the picture, refinancing can feel like a lifeline—or a failure. This book removes judgment from the conversation. Refinancing is not a sign of weakness. It is a financial tool. Like any tool, its value depends on how and why it is used. Borrowers deserve to understand their options without being rushed or made to feel uninformed.

Throughout this series, the goal has been to empower borrowers—not to turn them into loan officers, but to help them become informed participants in the mortgage process. FHA Refinance Options Made Simple continues that mission by breaking down each refinance path clearly and honestly. It explains what changes and what stays the same when you refinance, how lenders evaluate refinance applications, and why your loan balance, interest rate, and mortgage insurance matter more than most marketing materials admit.

This book also recognizes that refinancing does not happen in a vacuum. Life changes. Income changes. Family needs change. Markets change. FHA refinance options exist precisely because borrowers' lives are not static. Whether you are refinancing to create breathing room, improve cash flow, prepare for future goals, or simply regain peace of mind, the information in this book is designed to help you do so intentionally—not reactively.

Perhaps most importantly, this book encourages borrowers to think beyond the immediate monthly payment. While payment reduction is important, true financial progress comes from understanding long-term cost, total interest paid, loan duration, and opportunity cost. Refinancing should not just solve today's problem—it should support tomorrow's goals. That perspective is often missing in refinance conversations, and it is one of the central themes woven throughout this book.

As you read this foreword and move into the chapters that follow, approach refinancing not as a quick fix, but as a strategic decision point. Take your time. Reread sections if needed. Compare scenarios. Ask questions. A well-executed refinance can quietly improve your financial life year after year. A poorly executed one can silently cost tens of thousands of dollars. The difference is knowledge—and that is exactly what this book aims to provide.

Book 7 stands at a critical point in The FHA Homeownership & Wealth Series. It bridges the gap between owning a home and actively managing that ownership in a way that supports long-term stability and wealth. Whether you ultimately choose to refinance now, later, or not at all, the goal is for you to make that choice with clarity, confidence, and control. That is the foundation of smart homeownership—and the true purpose of this book.

Chapter 1

The Refinance Decision Point — When Refinancing Helps and When It Hurts

Refinancing is one of the most misunderstood moments in homeownership. Many borrowers believe refinancing is something you do when rates drop, when a lender calls, or when a new payment sounds appealing. In reality, refinancing is not a reaction—it is a decision point. It is the moment where a homeowner chooses whether to reset, restructure, or reinforce their financial position. With FHA loans, this decision carries even more weight because of how mortgage insurance, loan terms, and refinance rules interact over time. Understanding this decision point is the foundation for every refinance option discussed in this book.

At its core, refinancing replaces your existing mortgage with a new one. That sounds simple, but the implications are anything but. When you refinance, you are not just changing an interest rate—you are changing a timeline. You may be restarting a 30-year clock. You may be resetting mortgage insurance calculations. You may be trading short-term relief for long-term cost, or long-term stability for short-term flexibility. FHA refinance programs are designed to help borrowers, but they do not automatically help every borrower in every situation. The benefit comes from alignment, not availability.

One of the biggest mistakes homeowners make is assuming that a lower interest rate always equals savings. Interest rate is only one variable in a refinance equation. Loan balance, remaining term, upfront costs, monthly mortgage insurance, and how long you plan to keep the loan all matter just as much—sometimes more. FHA loans, in particular, require borrowers to think differently because mortgage insurance behaves differently than it does on conventional loans. Refinancing without understanding these mechanics can quietly increase total loan cost even when the monthly payment goes down.

Another common misconception is that refinancing is something lenders do for borrowers. In truth, refinancing is something borrowers must do for themselves—with intention. Lenders offer options, but borrowers live with the consequences. A refinance that looks good on paper may not support a borrower's real-world goals. Someone planning to stay in their home for twenty years needs a different strategy than someone planning to sell in five. Someone focused on monthly cash flow needs a different approach than someone focused on long-term equity growth. FHA refinance options exist to serve different needs, not to provide a one-size-fits-all solution. Timing plays a critical role in refinancing decisions. Refinancing too early can result in paying upfront mortgage insurance again before meaningful savings are realized. Refinancing too late can mean missing years of lower payments or interest savings. Many borrowers refinance based on headlines rather than personal math. They hear that rates dropped and assume action is required, without calculating whether the reduction offsets the cost of resetting their loan. FHA refinancing rewards patience and preparation more than urgency.

There is also an emotional component to refinancing that is rarely discussed. Homeowners often refinance during periods of stress—job changes, rising expenses, family transitions, or economic uncertainty. FHA refinance programs are intentionally designed to provide flexibility during these moments, but emotional decision-making can override long-term logic. This is why understanding refinance mechanics before you need them is so important. Clarity reduces pressure, and preparation prevents regret.

FHA refinancing falls into three primary categories: streamline refinance, rate-and-term refinance, and cash-out refinance. Each exists for a different reason, and each carries different trade-offs. The streamline refinance is designed for efficiency and payment reduction, not restructuring debt or accessing equity. The rate-and-term refinance is designed for strategic adjustments, such as changing loan length or removing a co-borrower. The cash-out refinance is designed for liquidity, not convenience. Confusing these purposes is where borrowers often run into trouble.

Another overlooked factor in refinancing is opportunity cost. Every refinance decision closes some doors while opening others. Resetting a loan term may reduce monthly payments but delay equity growth. Pulling cash out may solve a short-term need but reduce future borrowing power. FHA refinancing is powerful precisely because it gives borrowers options—but options only help when borrowers understand what they are giving up in exchange.

This chapter is not about convincing you to refinance. It is about teaching you how to evaluate whether refinancing serves your goals. Some of the smartest homeowners never refinance, even when rates drop, because their current loan structure already supports their long-term plan. Others refinance multiple times—but only when the math and timing align. The difference between smart refinancing and expensive refinancing is not access—it is understanding.

Before exploring specific FHA refinance programs in later chapters, borrowers must first understand their own position.

How much time remains on the loan. How much equity exists. How mortgage insurance affects total cost. How long the home is likely to be owned. Refinancing without answering these questions is like changing directions without knowing where you are going. FHA loans provide flexibility, but flexibility without strategy leads to drift.

Refinancing should be intentional, not impulsive. It should be driven by numbers, not noise. It should support both present needs and future goals. FHA refinance options were created to help borrowers adapt over time—not to trap them in perpetual resets. This chapter lays the foundation for every decision that follows by reframing refinancing as what it truly is: a strategic choice that deserves careful thought, honest math, and clear purpose.

The $312-a-Month Decision

Maria bought her home with an FHA loan five years ago. Her original purchase price was $280,000, and she put down 3.5 percent, financing $270,200 at a 4.75 percent interest rate. Her original monthly principal and interest payment was $1,410. With FHA mortgage insurance and escrow, her total monthly payment came to $1,865. At the time, the payment felt manageable, and owning a home felt like a victory.

Five years later, Maria's remaining loan balance was approximately $246,000. Interest rates had dropped, and she began receiving refinance offers promising to lower her payment by "over $300 per month." One lender offered an FHA streamline refinance at 3.25 percent. The new principal and interest payment would be $1,070. With mortgage insurance and escrow, her new total payment would be $1,553—saving her $312 per month.

At first glance, the decision seemed obvious. A $312 monthly savings meant $3,744 per year. Over five years, that would be $18,720 in reduced payments. The refinance required no appraisal and minimal documentation. Closing costs of $6,800 would be rolled into the new loan, increasing her balance to $252,800. Maria felt relieved. Lower payment. Less stress. Easy approval.

But Maria paused and ran the numbers.

Before refinancing, she had 25 years left on her loan. After refinancing, she would reset to a new 30-year term. While her payment dropped, her total interest over the life of the new loan would increase. On her existing loan, remaining interest over 25 years was approximately $164,000. On the new loan, total interest over 30 years would be about $190,000—an increase of $26,000 in long-term interest.

Maria then asked herself a critical question: how long would she keep the loan? If she planned to sell or refinance again within five years, the long-term interest increase would never fully materialize. Her $312 monthly savings over five years would outweigh the cost. But if she stayed in the home long-term, the math shifted. The refinance would provide short-term relief at the cost of long-term expense.

She also considered opportunity cost. By lowering her payment, she could redirect $312 per month into savings or debt reduction. Over five years, investing that amount—even conservatively—could create flexibility she didn't previously have. The refinance wasn't just about the mortgage. It was about cash flow and choice.

Maria ultimately decided to refinance—but with intention. She set a plan to apply the $312 monthly savings toward her principal balance for the first three years. By doing so, she would shorten the effective loan term and offset much of the long-term interest increase. The refinance became a tool, not a trap.

The numbers did not tell her what to do—but they gave her control over the decision. And that control made all the difference.

Chapter 2

The FHA Streamline Refinance — The Most Powerful Option Borrowers Rarely Fully Understand

The FHA Streamline Refinance is often described as the easiest refinance available, but "easy" can be misleading. While the process itself is simplified, the decision to use a streamline refinance requires careful thought. This program exists for one primary reason: to make an FHA borrower's mortgage more affordable. It was not designed to restructure debt, access equity, or reset financial goals. When used correctly, it can quietly improve a borrower's financial life with minimal friction. When misunderstood, it can lock borrowers into repeated resets that cost far more than they save.

The defining feature of the FHA streamline refinance is that it requires minimal documentation. No income verification is needed. No appraisal is required. Credit standards are more flexible than traditional refinancing. The program assumes that if a borrower has been making their FHA mortgage payments on time, they deserve an opportunity to benefit from lower interest rates. This borrower-friendly structure is intentional—but it also places more responsibility on the homeowner to evaluate whether the refinance truly makes sense.

One of the most important rules of the FHA streamline refinance is the net tangible benefit requirement. This rule exists to protect borrowers from refinancing simply for the sake of refinancing. In most cases, the new loan must reduce the monthly principal and interest payment by a meaningful amount or convert an adjustable rate to a fixed rate. However, meeting the technical requirement does not automatically mean the refinance is optimal. The rule measures immediate benefit, not long-term impact.

Another critical aspect of the streamline refinance is mortgage insurance. When an FHA loan is refinanced—streamline or otherwise—upfront mortgage insurance is typically charged again. While this cost can be rolled into the loan, it increases the loan balance and affects long-term interest. Many borrowers focus only on the monthly payment reduction and overlook how this upfront cost interacts with the loan term. Over time, this can dilute the savings they expected to achieve.

The streamline refinance is best suited for borrowers who plan to keep their home long enough to recapture the upfront cost but not so long that repeated refinances erase equity progress. It works exceptionally well for borrowers who secured their

FHA loan during periods of higher interest rates and have maintained consistent payment history. It is also ideal for homeowners seeking stability during uncertain times, as the simplified approval process reduces stress and uncertainty.

However, the streamline refinance is not a solution for every borrower. It does not allow cash-out. It does not permit major restructuring. It does not eliminate mortgage insurance. Borrowers looking to shorten their loan term, consolidate debt, or reposition their finances may find the streamline too limited. Understanding what the program does not do is just as important as understanding what it does.

Another common misunderstanding is the belief that skipping a mortgage payment creates savings. While some streamline refinances allow borrowers to defer a payment, that payment is not erased—it is simply absorbed into the new loan balance or closing costs. This can create temporary relief but should not be confused with true financial gain. Smart borrowers view this feature as a cash-flow tool, not free money.

Timing matters greatly with streamline refinances. Refinancing too soon after the original loan can result in minimal savings after costs are considered. Waiting too long can mean missing the most favorable interest rate environment. The FHA requires a seasoning period before a streamline refinance can occur, but meeting the minimum does not guarantee the timing is ideal. Borrowers benefit most when the interest rate reduction is substantial and expected to persist. The true power of the FHA streamline refinance lies in its simplicity—but simplicity does not mean carelessness. The program rewards borrowers who understand their numbers, their timeline, and their goals. It is not designed for constant optimization. It is designed for meaningful improvement. A single, well-timed streamline refinance can provide years of financial relief. Multiple poorly timed ones can quietly erode long-term wealth.

This chapter serves as a reminder that ease should never replace evaluation. The streamline refinance is a gift within the FHA system, but like all financial tools, its value depends on how it is used. Borrowers who approach it with clarity, patience, and math—not urgency—are the ones who benefit most.

The Two Streamlines, One Outcome

David purchased his home using an FHA loan at a 5.25 percent interest rate. His original loan amount was $310,000, and his monthly principal and interest payment was $1,713. With mortgage insurance and escrow, his total payment was $2,215. Two years into the loan, interest rates dropped sharply, and

David was offered an FHA streamline refinance at 3.75 percent.

The new payment calculation showed a principal and interest payment of $1,434. After mortgage insurance and escrow, his total payment dropped to $1,925—saving him $290 per month. Closing costs and upfront mortgage insurance totaling $7,500 were rolled into the loan, increasing his balance to $317,500. David accepted the refinance without hesitation. Over the next twelve months, the lower payment helped him stabilize his finances and rebuild savings.

One year later, rates dropped again. David received another streamline offer—this time at 3.25 percent. The projected payment would drop another $110 per month. His new loan balance would increase to $324,000 after costs. The math showed monthly savings, but David decided to pause.

He calculated his total savings from the first refinance: $290 per month for twelve months equaled $3,480. He then calculated the added loan balance from the first refinance: $7,500. While the refinance helped cash flow, it had not yet broken even. A second refinance would restart the clock again.

David compared scenarios. If he accepted the second refinance and saved $110 per month, it would take nearly six years to recapture the combined upfront costs. If he stayed in the home long-term, the numbers might work. But if he sold within five years, the second refinance would cost more than it saved.

David declined the second streamline refinance. Instead, he applied $110 per month toward principal on his existing loan. The decision did not feel exciting, but it was intentional. The first streamline gave him stability when he needed it. The second would have created diminishing returns.

By understanding the math behind “easy,” David avoided a refinance that looked beneficial on the surface but failed to support his long-term goals. The streamline worked—not because it was automatic, but because it was used with discipline.

Chapter 3

Rate-and-Term Refinancing — Rewriting the Loan Without Tapping Your Equity

While streamline refinances are designed for simplicity, the FHA rate-and-term refinance exists for borrowers who need flexibility without liquidation. This type of refinance allows homeowners to change the structure of their mortgage—interest rate, loan term, or both—without pulling cash out of their home. It is often the most misunderstood FHA refinance option because it looks similar to other refinances on the surface, yet behaves very differently beneath it. Rate-and-term refinancing is not about relief alone; it is about recalibration.

A rate-and-term refinance replaces an existing mortgage with a new one under revised terms. Borrowers may use it to lower their interest rate, shorten or extend their loan term, remove or add a borrower, or shift from an adjustable rate to a fixed rate. Unlike the streamline refinance, this option requires full documentation. Income must be verified. Credit must be reviewed. An appraisal is required. This additional scrutiny exists because the refinance fundamentally changes the risk profile of the loan. Many borrowers assume that a streamline refinance is always better because it is easier. In reality, the rate-and-term refinance often produces better long-term outcomes for borrowers with stable income and improving credit. While it requires more effort upfront, it provides more control. It allows borrowers to strategically reshape their mortgage instead of simply lowering a payment. This distinction is critical for homeowners who are thinking beyond short-term affordability.

One of the most common uses of a rate-and-term refinance is to shorten the loan term. Borrowers who initially chose a 30-year FHA loan for affordability may later refinance into a 20-year or 15-year term to accelerate equity growth. While this often increases the monthly payment, it dramatically reduces total interest paid over the life of the loan. This type of refinance shifts the focus from cash flow to wealth preservation and long-term efficiency.

Another frequent use is interest rate optimization when streamline guidelines are not favorable. Some borrowers may not meet the net tangible benefit requirement for a streamline refinance but can still benefit from a rate-and-term refinance. Others may have non-FHA loans they wish to refinance into FHA for stability or credit reasons. Rate-and-term refinancing offers flexibility where streamline refinances are restricted.

Mortgage insurance plays a central role in this decision. FHA mortgage insurance does not disappear with a rate-and-term refinance. In many cases, it resets. Borrowers must carefully calculate how the upfront mortgage insurance premium affects their loan balance and long-term cost. While the refinance may reduce interest rate or loan term, the added insurance cost can offset some of the savings if the refinance is not carefully structured.

This is where borrower intent becomes essential. Rate-and-term refinancing works best when the borrower has a clear objective. Refinancing without a defined goal often leads to marginal improvement at the expense of long-term efficiency. A borrower who refinances simply because a lender suggested it may gain little beyond cosmetic changes. A borrower who refinances with a plan can fundamentally improve their financial trajectory.

Another key consideration is loan seasoning and payment history. Because a rate-and-term refinance is fully underwritten, lenders will evaluate stability. This can work in the borrower's favor. Improved credit scores, increased income, or reduced debt can produce better pricing and lower rates. Unlike streamline refinances, which assume performance, rate-and-term refinances reward progress. There is also a psychological element to this type of refinance. It requires intention and patience. The paperwork is heavier. The timeline is longer. But the payoff is often clarity. Borrowers emerge with a loan that aligns with where they are now—not where they were when they first bought the home. For many homeowners, this refinance marks the transition from reactive borrowing to proactive financial management.

Rate-and-term refinancing is not for every borrower at every stage. It is not ideal for those seeking immediate relief or those planning to sell in the near future. It is best suited for homeowners with stable income, long-term ownership plans, and a desire to optimize their mortgage structure. When used correctly, it becomes a powerful tool for reshaping—not just reducing—the cost of homeownership.

This chapter exists to remind borrowers that not all refinances are about lowering payments. Some are about changing direction. A well-timed rate-and-term refinance can reduce years of interest, improve predictability, and create a mortgage that works in harmony with the borrower's broader financial goals. It is not the easiest path—but it is often the most intentional one.

The Fifteen-Year Pivot

Angela purchased her home with an FHA loan for $360,000 at a 4.875 percent interest rate. After her down payment, her initial loan amount was $347,400. Her monthly principal and interest payment on a 30-year term was $1,837. With mortgage insurance and escrow, her total payment was $2,385. At the time of purchase, the payment fit her budget and allowed her to adjust to homeownership comfortably.

Seven years later, Angela's remaining loan balance was approximately $301,000. Her income had increased significantly, her credit score had improved, and she no longer carried consumer debt. She was not struggling with her payment, but she felt uneasy knowing she still had over two decades left on her mortgage. She wanted control more than relief.

Angela explored a rate-and-term refinance into a 15-year FHA loan at 3.25 percent. The new loan would include $6,500 in closing costs and upfront mortgage insurance, rolled into the balance for a new total of $307,500. Her new monthly principal and interest payment would increase to $2,159. With mortgage insurance and escrow, her total payment would be $2,735—an increase of $350 per month.

At first glance, the refinance looked expensive. But Angela calculated the total interest. On her existing loan, remaining interest over the next 23 years would total approximately $192,000. On the new 15-year loan, total interest would be about $83,000. The refinance would save her nearly $109,000 in interest.

Angela then considered opportunity cost. The additional $350 per month felt manageable given her income growth. In exchange, she would own her home outright eight years sooner. The refinance wasn't about lowering expenses—it was about reclaiming time.

Angela accepted the refinance. The payment increase required adjustment, but the clarity it brought changed how she viewed her finances. Every payment now felt purposeful. The loan no longer lingered in the background of her life. It had an endpoint she could see.

The math didn't tell Angela what to value—but it showed her the trade. She chose control over comfort, and the rate-and-term refinance gave her exactly that.

Chapter 4

FHA Cash-Out Refinancing — Turning Equity into Opportunity Without Turning It into a Trap

Among all FHA refinance options, none is more powerful—or more dangerous—than the cash-out refinance. This is the point where homeownership moves beyond shelter and affordability and enters the realm of leverage. A cash-out refinance allows homeowners to convert a portion of their home equity into liquid cash, replacing their existing mortgage with a larger one. Used with discipline, this tool can eliminate high-interest debt, fund major life improvements, or create long-term financial leverage. Used without intention, it can quietly erase years of progress.

Equity represents stored value. It is not free money, and it is not income. It is wealth that exists because of time, appreciation, and consistent payments. An FHA cash-out refinance allows borrowers to access that stored value without selling their home, but it does so by reintroducing risk. The homeowner trades ownership percentage for liquidity. Understanding that trade is essential before moving forward. FHA cash-out refinances are governed by stricter rules than streamline or rate-and-term refinances. They require full income verification, credit review, appraisal, and adherence to loan-to-value limits. FHA typically allows cash-out refinances up to 80 percent of the home's appraised value, which means borrowers must retain at least 20 percent equity after the refinance. This safeguard exists to protect both the borrower and the loan system from over-leverage.

One of the most common mistakes borrowers make is focusing solely on the cash received instead of the new loan structure. The cash-out amount is only one piece of the equation. The interest rate, loan term reset, mortgage insurance, and increased balance all shape the long-term cost. Borrowers often celebrate receiving a large lump sum without fully accounting for how much that sum will cost over time.

Mortgage insurance plays an especially important role in FHA cash-out refinances. Because the loan balance increases, both upfront and monthly mortgage insurance costs rise. Even if the interest rate remains competitive, the added insurance expense can significantly affect total loan cost. Cash-out refinancing should therefore be evaluated not only as a borrowing decision, but as a long-term financing commitment.

Intent separates productive cash-out refinances from destructive ones. Borrowers who use cash-out proceeds to pay off high-interest debt often improve their net financial position, even if their mortgage balance increases. Replacing 18 percent credit card debt with a 5 percent mortgage rate can reduce total interest dramatically. However, this only works if spending habits change. Using home equity to erase unsecured debt without addressing the behavior that created it often leads to reaccumulation—and deeper financial strain.

Cash-out refinances are also commonly used for home improvements. When the improvements add measurable value or reduce future expenses, the refinance can strengthen the homeowner's position. Structural repairs, energy efficiency upgrades, or additions that increase usable space can justify the leverage. Cosmetic upgrades that do not improve value or function may feel satisfying, but they rarely justify the long-term cost of borrowed equity.

Another increasingly common use of FHA cash-out refinances is funding business ventures or investments. This strategy requires the highest level of discipline. Borrowers must understand that they are converting a secured asset—their home—into capital that carries risk. While some investments generate returns that exceed mortgage interest, others do not. The home should never be treated as a casual source of funding. It is the foundation of financial stability, not a revolving credit line. Timing is critical with cash-out refinances. Pulling equity too early limits future flexibility. Waiting too long may mean missing favorable rates or appreciation cycles. Borrowers should evaluate not only current needs, but future borrowing plans. A cash-out refinance reduces available equity for future refinances, sales proceeds, or emergency access. This opportunity cost must be weighed carefully.

There is also an emotional component to cash-out decisions. Receiving a large sum of money can create a false sense of abundance. Without a clear plan, the funds can disappear quickly while the larger mortgage remains for decades. This is why FHA cash-out refinancing should always begin with a written purpose, a defined amount, and a repayment mindset—even though the loan does not require repayment beyond the mortgage itself.

When used correctly, the FHA cash-out refinance becomes a strategic bridge. It allows homeowners to reposition their finances, consolidate obligations, and deploy capital intentionally. When used poorly, it becomes a silent setback that delays wealth building and increases vulnerability. The difference lies in preparation, math, and restraint.

This chapter is not meant to discourage cash-out refinancing. It is meant to elevate it. FHA cash-out refinances are not shortcuts—they are tools. And tools demand respect. Borrowers who approach them with clarity and caution often unlock opportunities that would otherwise remain inaccessible. Those who rush in without understanding the trade often spend years trying to recover lost ground.

Equity with a Plan

Marcus purchased his home eight years ago using an FHA loan. The original purchase price was $295,000, and his initial loan amount was $284,675. His interest rate was 4.625 percent, and his monthly principal and interest payment was $1,464. Over the years, Marcus made consistent payments and benefited from rising home values in his area.

When Marcus considered refinancing, his home appraised for $420,000. His remaining loan balance was approximately $246,000. Under FHA guidelines, he could refinance up to 80 percent of the home's value, or $336,000. This meant he could potentially access about $90,000 in equity after paying off the existing loan and closing costs.

The new FHA cash-out refinance offered a 5.25 percent interest rate. After including $9,000 in upfront mortgage insurance and closing costs, Marcus's new loan amount would be $336,000. His new monthly principal and interest payment would increase to $1,856. With mortgage insurance and escrow, his total payment would rise by $410 per month. At first, the increase concerned him. But Marcus listed his current debts. He had $38,000 in credit card balances at an average interest rate of 19 percent, costing him roughly $600 per month in minimum payments. He also had a $22,000 auto loan at 7.5 percent with a $425 monthly payment. By using $60,000 of the cash-out proceeds to eliminate these debts, Marcus would free up $1,025 per month.

After refinancing, his mortgage payment increased by $410, but his eliminated debts reduced his expenses by $1,025. His net monthly cash flow improved by $615. Over five years, that improvement would total $36,900—far exceeding the upfront cost of refinancing.

Marcus set aside the remaining $30,000 as a reserve fund, not spending it immediately. He treated the refinance as a restructuring, not a windfall. The math justified the decision because the purpose was clear and controlled.

The cash-out refinance didn't make Marcus richer overnight. But it made his financial structure stronger. Equity wasn't consumed—it was redeployed with intention. And that made all the difference.

Chapter 5

Cash-Out or Cash Trap — How FHA Equity Decisions Shape Your Financial Future

The moment a homeowner considers a cash-out refinance, the conversation changes. Refinancing is no longer just about interest rates or monthly payments—it becomes a question of leverage, responsibility, and long-term consequence. An FHA cash-out refinance allows borrowers to convert a portion of their home equity into usable cash while keeping ownership of the property. This capability can be life-changing, but it also introduces a level of risk that does not exist with other refinance options. Equity, once removed from the home, does not quietly return on its own.

Home equity is created slowly. It builds through monthly payments, appreciation, and time. A cash-out refinance compresses that time by turning years of accumulated value into immediate liquidity. This trade can be beneficial, but it must be treated with respect. FHA loans are designed to promote stability, not speculation. The cash-out option exists to support meaningful financial restructuring—not impulsive consumption. FHA cash-out refinances differ from streamline and rate-and-term refinances in both intent and structure. They require full documentation, including income verification, credit review, and a new appraisal. The FHA also limits how much equity can be accessed, generally capping the new loan at eighty percent of the home's appraised value. This limitation is intentional. It forces borrowers to retain a buffer of equity, protecting them from market fluctuations and overextension.

One of the most overlooked consequences of a cash-out refinance is the resetting of financial momentum. When equity is removed, the loan balance increases, and in most cases, the loan term resets to thirty years. While the borrower gains immediate access to cash, they also extend the timeline of repayment. This tradeoff is rarely discussed openly, yet it plays a major role in determining whether a cash-out refinance supports or undermines long-term wealth.

Mortgage insurance further complicates the equation. FHA mortgage insurance is recalculated based on the new, higher loan balance. Even if the interest rate is reasonable, the combined effect of interest, mortgage insurance, and extended repayment can make cash-out borrowing far more expensive than it appears on the surface. Borrowers must evaluate not only how much cash they receive, but how much that cash will ultimately cost. The purpose of the cash-out refinance matters more than the amount. Borrowers who use equity to eliminate high-interest debt often improve their financial structure, even though their mortgage balance increases. The key is that the refinance replaces expensive, unstable debt with lower-cost, predictable debt. However, this benefit only exists if the behavior that caused the debt changes. Without discipline, borrowers risk turning their home into a revolving credit source—one that is far harder to recover from.

Cash-out refinancing is also frequently used to fund home improvements. When those improvements add measurable value or reduce long-term expenses, the refinance can strengthen the homeowner's position. Structural upgrades, energy efficiency improvements, or necessary repairs often justify the use of equity. Conversely, lifestyle upgrades that do not enhance value may feel rewarding in the short term but often fail the long-term math test.

Some borrowers consider using FHA cash-out proceeds to fund business ventures or investments. This strategy demands the highest level of caution. A home is a secured asset, while investments carry varying degrees of risk. When equity is converted into capital, the borrower assumes that the return will exceed the cost of borrowing. Sometimes it does. Sometimes it does not. The home, however, remains on the line either way. Timing is another critical factor. Pulling equity during a strong market can feel safe, but markets change. A cash-out refinance reduces the homeowner's margin of safety. If values decline or income changes, the borrower may find themselves with fewer options. FHA's equity limits exist to mitigate this risk, but they do not eliminate it entirely. Borrowers must think beyond today's appraisal and consider tomorrow's uncertainty.

The psychological impact of receiving a large sum of money should not be underestimated. Cash-out proceeds can feel like a reward for years of responsible ownership. Without a clear plan, however, the funds often disappear quickly, while the larger mortgage remains. This disconnect is what turns opportunity into regret. Successful cash-out refinances begin with a defined purpose, a capped amount, and a long-term mindset.

An FHA cash-out refinance is neither good nor bad on its own. It is a multiplier. It amplifies discipline or amplifies risk, depending on how it is used. Borrowers who approach it strategically can reshape their finances, reduce stress, and create flexibility. Borrowers who approach it emotionally often sacrifice future stability for present comfort. Understanding this distinction is essential before proceeding. This chapter exists to slow the decision down. FHA cash-out refinancing should never be rushed. It should be evaluated with clear math, realistic assumptions, and an honest assessment of behavior and goals. Equity is one of the most powerful assets a homeowner has. Using it wisely can accelerate progress. Using it carelessly can undo years of effort.

The $78,000 Reallocation

Sonia purchased her home with an FHA loan nine years ago for $310,000. After her down payment, her original loan balance was $299,150 at an interest rate of 4.5 percent. Her monthly principal and interest payment was $1,516. Over time, Sonia's income increased, but so did her financial obligations. She accumulated credit card debt and took out a personal loan during a difficult period, believing she would "catch up later."

When Sonia reviewed her finances, her home appraised for $455,000. Her remaining mortgage balance was approximately $248,000. Under FHA guidelines, she could refinance up to eighty percent of the home's value, or $364,000. After accounting for closing costs and mortgage insurance, she could access roughly $78,000 in cash.

The new FHA cash-out refinance carried a 5.375 percent interest rate. Sonia's new loan balance would be $364,000, and her new principal and interest payment would rise to $2,038. Including mortgage insurance and escrow, her total payment increased by $470 per month. At first, the increase alarmed her. But Sonia listed her existing debts. She had $42,000 in credit card balances at an average interest rate of 21 percent, costing her nearly $880 per month. She also had a $19,000 personal loan with a $390 monthly payment. By using $61,000 of the cash-out proceeds to eliminate those debts, Sonia reduced her monthly obligations by $1,270.

After refinancing, her housing payment increased by $470, but her eliminated debts reduced expenses by $1,270. Her net monthly improvement was $800. Over three years, that improvement would total $28,800—far exceeding the refinance costs.

Sonia did not spend the remaining $17,000. She placed it in a separate account designated as a reserve. The refinance was not a reward—it was a reallocation. Equity was given a job, not an invitation.

The math didn't promise comfort. It required discipline. But by treating the cash-out refinance as a structural reset rather than a financial windfall, Sonia turned accumulated equity into long-term stability instead of long-term strain.

Chapter 6

The Hidden Cost of "Yes" — When Refinancing Quietly Makes Things Worse

Refinancing is often presented as a solution, but not every solution improves the problem it claims to fix. One of the most expensive mistakes FHA borrowers make is refinancing when the numbers technically work, but the outcome quietly undermines their financial position. These are not reckless decisions. They are reasonable decisions made without full context. Chapter 5 exists to illuminate the moments when refinancing looks helpful on the surface but erodes progress underneath.

The most common refinance mistake is focusing on monthly payment reduction while ignoring total loan cost. A lower payment can feel like relief, especially during periods of financial pressure, but relief is not the same as improvement. When a refinance extends the loan term, resets mortgage insurance, and increases the balance through rolled-in costs, the borrower may pay far more over time—even while enjoying short-term savings. FHA loans, because of their structure, make this trade-off especially easy to overlook. Loan term resets are among the most underestimated consequences of refinancing. A borrower ten years into a 30-year loan who refinances into a new 30-year term effectively adds ten years of interest payments back onto the loan. Even with a lower rate, the extended timeline can increase total interest paid dramatically. FHA refinance programs allow this because they prioritize affordability, but affordability without perspective can become a long-term liability.

Mortgage insurance magnifies this effect. FHA mortgage insurance does not disappear simply because a borrower refinances. In many cases, it restarts. This means borrowers who refinance multiple times may pay upfront mortgage insurance repeatedly while extending monthly insurance costs. Over time, this can add tens of thousands of dollars to the cost of homeownership—costs that rarely appear in refinance marketing.

Another hidden cost of refinancing is opportunity loss. Every refinance decision limits future options. Rolling closing costs into the loan reduces equity. Pulling cash out reduces borrowing capacity. Resetting the loan term delays the point at which the home becomes a low-cost or debt-free asset. These costs do not show up on monthly statements, but they shape long-term flexibility. Behavior also plays a decisive role. Refinancing to solve a cash-flow issue without addressing spending habits often creates a temporary improvement followed by deeper strain. FHA refinance programs are not behavioral tools—they are structural tools. They change the shape of debt, not the behaviors that create it. When borrowers rely on refinancing as a recurring fix, they slowly convert equity into a revolving resource that becomes harder to replenish.

Market timing mistakes further compound these issues. Borrowers who refinance at the peak of rate cycles or rush to lock in marginal improvements often find themselves stuck when better opportunities emerge later. FHA refinancing rewards patience more than urgency. A refinance that saves $50 per month may meet program guidelines, but it rarely justifies the cost and reset involved.

There are also situations where refinancing simply does not align with the borrower's timeline. Homeowners planning to sell within a few years often fail to recover refinance costs before exiting the property. FHA loans are not designed for rapid turnover. Refinancing without considering the likely length of ownership can turn a well-intentioned decision into an unnecessary expense.

This chapter is not meant to discourage refinancing. It is meant to restore balance to the conversation. FHA refinance options are powerful, but power without restraint produces diminishing returns. The best refinance decisions are often the ones borrowers choose not to make—at least not yet.

Understanding when not to refinance is just as important as understanding how to refinance. Sometimes the smartest move is to stay put, continue paying down the existing loan, and preserve equity for a more meaningful opportunity. In those moments, restraint becomes a form of strategy.

Refinancing should move a borrower forward, not sideways. If the decision does not clearly improve stability, reduce risk, or support long-term goals, it deserves a pause. FHA programs offer flexibility, but flexibility must be matched with judgment. This chapter exists to help borrowers recognize when a polite "no" is the most financially responsible answer.

Saving $180 That Cost a Decade

Jonathan purchased his home with an FHA loan at age thirty-two. The purchase price was $265,000, and his original loan balance was $255,725 at an interest rate of 4.25 percent. His monthly principal and interest payment was $1,257. Ten years later, Jonathan's remaining loan balance was approximately $207,000. He had built solid equity and rarely thought about refinancing because his payment felt manageable. When rates dropped, Jonathan was offered a streamline refinance at 3.5 percent. The lender showed him a new monthly payment of $1,077—saving him $180 per month. Closing costs and mortgage insurance totaling $8,900 would be rolled into the new loan, increasing his balance to $216,000. Jonathan accepted the refinance without hesitation.

What Jonathan did not calculate was the timeline reset. Before refinancing, he had twenty years remaining on his loan. After refinancing, he returned to a thirty-year term. While the rate was lower, the extended repayment period changed the math dramatically.

On his original loan, Jonathan's remaining interest over twenty years would have been approximately $92,000. On the new loan, total interest over thirty years would be roughly $161,000. The refinance increased his total interest cost by nearly $69,000.

Jonathan enjoyed the $180 monthly savings and used it for discretionary spending rather than principal reduction. Five years later, he refinanced again, chasing another small payment reduction. Each decision felt harmless. Each one extended the timeline further.

At age fifty-five, Jonathan realized he still had a mortgage payment he expected to be finished years earlier. The refinance never felt like a mistake because it never hurt in the moment. It simply delayed the future—quietly and consistently.

The math didn't punish Jonathan immediately. It waited. And by the time he noticed, the cost was already embedded in time he couldn't recover.

Chapter 7

The Right Refinance at the Right Time — Matching FHA Options to Your Life Stage

Refinancing decisions rarely fail because of math alone. They fail because they are made without context. FHA refinance programs are designed to support borrowers at different stages of life, yet many homeowners choose options that solve yesterday's problem or create tomorrow's constraint. Understanding which refinance aligns with your current life stage is one of the most important skills a homeowner can develop. The right refinance at the wrong time can be just as damaging as the wrong refinance altogether.

Life stages shape financial priorities. Early in homeownership, affordability and stability often matter more than optimization. Borrowers may be adjusting to new expenses, career growth, or family changes. In this stage, refinance decisions should preserve flexibility and avoid unnecessary resets. Streamline refinances, when used carefully, can offer breathing room without complexity. Rate-and-term or cash-out refinances at this stage often do more harm than good unless driven by a clear structural need. Mid-stage homeowners face a different set of considerations. Income may be more stable, credit stronger, and equity meaningful. This is where refinancing becomes a strategic tool rather than a survival tool. Borrowers in this phase may benefit from rate-and-term refinances to shorten loan duration or optimize interest cost. The focus shifts from monthly relief to long-term efficiency. FHA refinance programs can support this shift, but only if borrowers resist the temptation to reset for convenience.

Later-stage homeowners often approach refinancing with a different mindset altogether. The mortgage is no longer just a payment—it is a timeline. Refinancing late in the loan without considering remaining years can delay retirement plans, restrict cash flow later in life, or convert a nearly paid-off home into a long-term obligation. At this stage, refinancing should be approached conservatively. Any refinance should have a clear payoff horizon and a defined benefit that outweighs the cost of resetting progress.

Family dynamics also influence refinance decisions. Growing households may prioritize space and cash flow, while downsizing households may prioritize predictability and debt reduction. FHA refinance options can support both, but they must be matched intentionally. A cash-out refinance to fund education or consolidate debt may make sense during peak earning years, but the same decision late in life may introduce unnecessary risk.

Career stability is another factor that often gets overlooked. Borrowers with variable income may benefit from the simplicity of streamline refinances during uncertain periods, while borrowers with predictable income may benefit more from rate-and-term refinances that lock in efficiency. FHA programs offer flexibility, but flexibility works best when it aligns with income patterns, not just interest rates.

Market conditions also intersect with life stage. Refinancing during favorable rate environments can amplify good decisions or soften bad ones, but market timing should never override personal timing. A refinance that looks attractive in the market may be inappropriate for a borrower nearing a major life transition. FHA refinance options exist to support borrowers, not to push them into decisions that feel urgent but lack alignment.

One of the most important principles of life-stage refinancing is understanding when not to act. Sometimes the smartest move is to continue paying the existing loan and allow equity and time to do their work. Refinancing should not be a reflex. It should be a response to a meaningful shift in circumstances, goals, or opportunity. Borrowers who treat refinancing as a recurring event often lose sight of the bigger picture. FHA loans are long-term instruments. Refinancing too frequently, even when technically beneficial, can fragment progress and erode momentum. Each refinance should move the borrower closer to a defined outcome, not simply create short-term comfort.

This chapter encourages borrowers to view refinancing as a chapter in a longer story, not an isolated decision. The goal is not to find the "best" refinance in abstract terms, but the right refinance for where you are now—and where you intend to be next. FHA refinance programs are tools, not destinations. Their value is determined by alignment, timing, and intention.

Understanding your life stage does not guarantee the perfect decision, but it dramatically reduces the risk of regret. Refinancing becomes less about chasing numbers and more about supporting the life you are building. That shift in perspective is what turns FHA refinance options into strategic assets rather than recurring distractions.

Timing the Life, Not the Rate

Elena bought her home with an FHA loan at age thirty-five. The purchase price was $330,000, and her original loan balance was $318,450 at an interest rate of 4.625 percent. Her monthly principal and interest payment was $1,638. At the time, she was early in her career and focused on stability rather than optimization.

Eight years later, Elena's income had increased, and her remaining loan balance was approximately $267,000. Interest rates dropped, and she was offered a streamline refinance that would lower her payment by $140 per month. Closing costs and mortgage insurance totaling $7,800 would be rolled into the new loan, increasing her balance to $274,800.

Elena paused. She calculated her timeline. She planned to sell the home within four years to relocate closer to family. Saving $140 per month over four years would total $6,720—less than the cost of refinancing. The refinance looked helpful but failed the timing test.

Two years later, Elena's plans changed. She decided to stay long-term. Rates dropped again, and this time she explored a rate-and-term refinance into a 20-year FHA loan at 3.25 percent. The new loan balance, including costs, would be $271,000. Her new principal and interest payment would increase slightly to $1,705.

Elena ran the math. On her existing loan, remaining interest over twenty-two years would total approximately $181,000. On the new loan, total interest over twenty years would be about $96,000. The refinance would save her roughly $85,000 in interest. The payment increase was manageable given her income growth. The refinance aligned with her new life stage. The same refinance that didn't make sense two years earlier became the right move later—not because the numbers changed dramatically, but because her life did.

Elena didn't time the market. She timed her decision. And that made all the difference.

Chapter 8

Timing the Rate or Timing Your Life — Why the Best Refinance Isn't Always the Lowest Rate

One of the most persistent myths in mortgage lending is that refinancing success is determined by interest rates alone. Borrowers are conditioned to believe that the lowest available rate automatically represents the smartest decision. In reality, interest rate is only one variable in a much larger equation. FHA refinance programs were designed to serve real people living real lives, not spreadsheets frozen in time. The most effective refinance decisions are rarely made by chasing the market; they are made by aligning the loan with the borrower's life.

Interest rates move constantly, but life moves in phases. Careers change. Families grow or contract. Health, priorities, and financial resilience evolve. Refinancing based solely on rate movements assumes that everything else remains static. This assumption is rarely true. FHA borrowers who refinance strictly because rates drop often discover that the savings they expected fail to materialize in meaningful ways once closing costs, loan resets, and timing are considered. Rate timing encourages urgency. Life timing encourages intention. Borrowers who wait for the perfect rate often miss the opportunity to restructure their loan when it would have the greatest impact. Others rush into refinances that look optimal in the moment but create long-term misalignment. FHA refinancing rewards clarity more than precision. A refinance executed at the right moment in a borrower's life can outperform a technically better refinance done at the wrong time.

One of the clearest examples of this tension is loan term selection. Borrowers may qualify for a lower rate by extending the loan term, but doing so late in the loan cycle can delay financial independence. Conversely, refinancing into a shorter term at a slightly higher rate may accelerate wealth building and reduce total cost. The "better" rate depends entirely on the borrower's timeline, not the market's headline.

Cash-out refinancing further highlights this distinction. Pulling equity during a favorable rate environment can seem prudent, but if the borrower's income is unstable or future plans are uncertain, the refinance may introduce risk that outweighs the benefit. FHA cash-out options exist to support meaningful transitions—not to capitalize on short-term market conditions. Timing equity access with life stability often matters more than timing it with rates. Borrowers also underestimate the cost of waiting. Waiting for rates to drop another quarter-point can cost months or years of lost opportunity. If a refinance improves cash flow, reduces stress, or supports a strategic shift, delaying it may have a greater cost than the marginal rate improvement would save. FHA refinancing is about outcomes, not perfection.

This does not mean borrowers should ignore rates altogether. Rates matter. They influence affordability and long-term cost. But they should be evaluated within context. A refinance that reduces risk, increases predictability, or supports a major life transition may be worth pursuing even if rates are not at historic lows. FHA programs exist to create stability, not to reward speculation.

Another overlooked factor is psychological timing. Financial decisions made during high-stress periods often prioritize immediate relief over long-term benefit. Conversely, decisions made during stable periods allow for strategic thinking. FHA refinancing works best when borrowers are not reacting, but planning. This requires awareness not only of market conditions, but of personal readiness.

Life timing also affects how long a borrower will benefit from a refinance. A homeowner planning to relocate, retire, or change household structure must evaluate whether the refinance timeline aligns with those plans. FHA refinance programs are flexible, but flexibility does not override math. A refinance must have time to work in the borrower's favor. This chapter challenges the idea that there is a single right time to refinance. Instead, it introduces the concept of personal timing. The right refinance occurs when the borrower's goals, stability, and plans align with the loan structure—not when the market briefly offers an attractive number. FHA refinancing becomes a strategic advantage when borrowers prioritize alignment over optimization.

Ultimately, refinancing is a life decision disguised as a financial one. Interest rates will always change. Life will always evolve. Borrowers who recognize this dynamic gain an advantage. They stop chasing numbers and start shaping outcomes. FHA refinance options provide the flexibility to do just that—when used at the right moment.

The Rate She Didn't Chase

Danielle purchased her home with an FHA loan for $345,000 at an interest rate of 4.75 percent. Her original loan balance was $332,925, and her monthly principal and interest payment was $1,737. Over time, Danielle's career progressed, and her income stabilized. Seven years into the loan, her remaining balance was approximately $281,000.

When interest rates dropped to 3.75 percent, Danielle was offered a streamline refinance. The refinance would lower her payment by $185 per month. Closing costs and mortgage insurance totaling $8,200 would be rolled into the loan, increasing her balance to $289,200. The numbers worked, but Danielle hesitated. She was planning to start her own business within a year, which would temporarily reduce her income.

Six months later, rates dropped another quarter-point to 3.5 percent. Danielle was encouraged to wait even longer. But instead of waiting, she evaluated her life timing. She wanted predictable expenses before making her career transition. She accepted the refinance at 3.75 percent.

The refinance saved her $185 per month, or $2,220 per year. Over three years, that savings would total $6,660. If she had waited for the lower rate, the additional savings would have been only $35 per month—$1,260 over three years. But waiting would have cost her six months of savings, or $1,110.

By acting when her life required stability rather than perfection, Danielle came out ahead. The quarter-point she didn't chase never mattered. What mattered was alignment.

Danielle didn't time the market. She timed her transition. And that decision gave her control when she needed it most.

Chapter 9

Building Wealth Without Overleveraging — How FHA Refinancing Becomes a Long-Term Asset

Wealth is rarely built through dramatic moves. It is built through controlled decisions repeated over time. FHA refinancing, when used intentionally, can support this process by improving cash flow, restructuring debt, and preserving flexibility. When used aggressively or emotionally, it can do the opposite. The difference between wealth-building and wealth erosion lies not in the refinance itself, but in how leverage is managed.

Leverage amplifies outcomes. It magnifies discipline or magnifies risk. FHA refinance programs provide access to leverage through reduced payments, extended terms, or equity extraction. None of these are inherently negative. The danger appears when leverage is used to compensate for weak planning or unstable behavior. Wealth-focused refinancing prioritizes sustainability over speed.

One of the most effective wealth-building uses of FHA refinancing is cash-flow optimization. Lowering a payment without resetting progress excessively allows borrowers to redirect capital toward savings, investing, or accelerated principal reduction. This strategy works best when the borrower commits the freed cash flow intentionally. Without commitment, the benefit dissolves into lifestyle inflation.

Another powerful use of refinancing is interest efficiency. Refinancing to a shorter term or lower rate can reduce total interest paid by tens or even hundreds of thousands of dollars. This is wealth preservation in its purest form. It does not feel exciting, but it compounds quietly. FHA rate-and-term refinances are particularly effective for borrowers who have reached income stability and want to reclaim time from their mortgage.

Equity access can also play a role in wealth building—but only under strict conditions. Using FHA cash-out refinancing to fund appreciating assets or eliminate high-interest liabilities can improve net worth. Using equity to fund consumption almost always reduces it. Wealth builders treat equity as capital with accountability, not as a convenience.

Overleveraging is the primary threat. Borrowers who repeatedly refinance, extract equity, or reset loan terms often mistake motion for progress. Each refinance should move the borrower closer to a defined outcome: lower risk, greater flexibility, or faster payoff. If the refinance does not clearly serve one of these purposes, it likely increases leverage without increasing wealth.

Another key principle is margin preservation. FHA loans require mortgage insurance and enforce loan-to-value limits for a reason. These constraints protect borrowers from themselves. Maintaining a healthy equity buffer preserves optionality. It allows borrowers to weather market downturns, income disruptions, or unexpected expenses without panic refinancing or forced sales.

Wealth-focused refinancing also accounts for life transitions. Borrowers approaching retirement, business ownership, or geographic changes must think defensively. Reducing debt exposure and increasing predictability often matter more than maximizing leverage. FHA refinancing can support this shift, but only if borrowers resist the temptation to optimize every dollar.

Tax implications, while often secondary, should not be ignored. Mortgage interest deductions, opportunity costs, and asset allocation all intersect with refinancing decisions. Wealth is holistic. FHA refinancing touches only one part of the financial picture, but its effects ripple outward.

The most successful borrowers treat refinancing as a system, not an event. They evaluate each decision against long-term goals. They avoid unnecessary resets. They protect equity. They use leverage sparingly and purposefully. FHA refinancing becomes a quiet partner in wealth creation—not a recurring distraction.

This chapter is not about extracting maximum value from a loan. It is about preserving financial resilience while allowing growth. Wealth is built when borrowers remain in control. FHA refinance programs, when used with restraint, help borrowers maintain that control while steadily improving their financial position.

Turning $240 into $96,000

Calvin purchased his home with an FHA loan for $380,000. After his down payment, his original loan balance was $366,700 at an interest rate of 4.875 percent. His monthly principal and interest payment was $1,940. Eight years later, his remaining balance was approximately $314,000. Calvin was financially stable and considering long-term strategies rather than short-term relief.

Calvin refinanced using a rate-and-term FHA refinance into a 20-year loan at 3.375 percent. Closing costs and mortgage insurance totaling $8,600 were rolled into the loan, bringing the new balance to $322,600. His new principal and interest payment increased to $2,180—an increase of $240 per month.

Instead of viewing the increase as a burden, Calvin evaluated the trade. On his existing loan, remaining interest over twenty-two years would have totaled approximately $228,000. On the new loan, total interest over twenty years would be about $132,000. The refinance reduced his interest cost by $96,000.

Calvin committed to the strategy. He treated the higher payment as an investment, not an expense. The additional $240 per month secured him eight fewer years of mortgage payments and nearly six figures in preserved wealth.

The refinance did not give Calvin cash in hand. It gave him certainty, efficiency, and time. By avoiding overleveraging and focusing on long-term structure, Calvin used FHA refinancing to quietly improve his net worth—without extracting a single dollar of equity.

The math did not excite him. It convinced him. And that conviction paid dividends long after the paperwork was signed.

Chapter 10

House Hacking and Multi-Unit Refinancing — Using FHA Without Turning Your Home into a Risk Asset

FHA loans occupy a unique space in real estate because they allow owner-occupants to purchase and live in multi-unit properties while using rental income to offset housing costs. When refinancing enters this picture, the stakes increase. A refinance on a single-family home affects one household. A refinance on a multi-unit property affects cash flow, tenant stability, and long-term investment performance. FHA refinancing in this context must be approached as both a housing decision and a business decision.

House hacking with FHA loans often begins with simplicity. A borrower buys a two- to four-unit property, lives in one unit, and rents out the others. Early on, the goal is survival and stability—covering the mortgage, learning property management basics, and adjusting to shared ownership dynamics. Refinancing during this early phase can be dangerous if driven by optimism rather than performance. FHA refinance options reward proven stability, not projected income. As rental income becomes consistent, refinancing opportunities expand. Borrowers may consider streamline refinances to reduce payments and improve cash flow. In multi-unit situations, even modest payment reductions can materially improve monthly margins. However, borrowers must remember that FHA streamline refinances do not reassess rental income. The benefit is purely structural. If the property's cash flow is fragile, the refinance may provide relief without addressing underlying risk.

Rate-and-term refinancing introduces a different layer of complexity. In multi-unit properties, appraisals matter more. Market rents, occupancy rates, and property condition directly influence valuation. A rate-and-term refinance can be an opportunity to restructure the loan once the property has proven itself. Borrowers who initially chose longer terms for affordability may later shorten terms to accelerate equity growth—especially when rental income offsets the payment increase.

Cash-out refinancing in multi-unit FHA properties demands the highest level of discipline. Pulling equity from a property that supports housing and income simultaneously introduces leverage on both fronts. If rental income declines, the borrower remains responsible for the larger payment. FHA guidelines limit cash-out exposure for a reason. Multi-unit borrowers must maintain margin not just for market risk, but for tenant risk.

One of the most common mistakes multi-unit FHA borrowers make is treating rental income as guaranteed. Refinancing decisions based on full occupancy assume ideal conditions. Vacancies, maintenance, and turnover are not hypothetical—they are inevitable. Refinancing must be structured to survive imperfection. FHA programs are forgiving, but lenders and markets are not.

Another overlooked factor is lifestyle tolerance. Living in a multi-unit property is different from owning a single-family home. Noise, maintenance, and tenant relationships affect quality of life. Refinancing to maximize leverage while minimizing personal margin often leads to burnout. FHA refinancing should support sustainability, not strain it.

Borrowers must also consider exit strategy. FHA loans are owner-occupied by design. Refinancing into FHA products assumes continued occupancy. Borrowers planning to move out must evaluate whether refinancing aligns with future conversion plans. Refinancing without considering the eventual transition from owner-occupant to investor can limit options.

Successful multi-unit refinancing balances three priorities: housing stability, cash-flow resilience, and equity growth. FHA refinance options can support all three, but only when decisions are grounded in actual performance rather than projections. Borrowers who treat their property as a system—not a shortcut—are far more likely to succeed.

This chapter emphasizes caution not because opportunity is limited, but because opportunity compounds risk when misused. FHA refinancing in a multi-unit context is powerful. It can reduce living expenses, accelerate wealth creation, and provide leverage responsibly. But it requires patience, math, and realism.

House hacking is not passive income in the early years. Refinancing should reflect that reality. When structured conservatively, FHA refinancing strengthens both the home and the investment. When structured aggressively, it puts both at risk. The difference lies in margin, not ambition.

Cash Flow Before Leverage

Ryan purchased a duplex using an FHA loan for $420,000. After his down payment, his loan balance was $405,300 at an interest rate of 4.75 percent. His monthly principal and interest payment was $2,115. With mortgage insurance and escrow, his total housing payment was $2,780.

Ryan lived in one unit and rented the other for $1,850 per month. After utilities and maintenance averaging $300, his net offset was $1,550. His effective housing cost was $1,230 per month, which felt manageable.

Three years later, the property appraised for $495,000. Ryan's remaining loan balance was approximately $368,000. He considered a cash-out refinance up to 80 percent of value, which would allow a new loan of $396,000. After closing costs, he could access about $20,000 in equity.

The new FHA cash-out refinance would raise his total monthly payment to $3,050—an increase of $270 per month. Ryan ran the numbers. His rental income had been stable, but turnover had already cost him one month of rent during the previous year. One vacancy under the new payment structure would erase months of gains.

Instead of cashing out, Ryan chose a streamline refinance that reduced his payment by $180 per month. His new effective housing cost dropped to $1,050. Over two years, the savings totaled $4,320. Combined with appreciation and loan paydown, his equity position improved without added risk.

Ryan postponed leverage until performance justified it. The duplex didn't need extraction—it needed breathing room. By prioritizing cash flow over cash-out, he preserved flexibility and avoided turning a solid housing strategy into a fragile one.

The math didn't tell Ryan what he could do. It showed him what he could survive. And that perspective changed everything.

Chapter 11

The Borrower's Refinance Framework – Turning Information into Confident Action

By the time a borrower reaches the end of this book, the mechanics of FHA refinancing should no longer feel mysterious. Streamline refinances, rate-and-term refinances, and cash-out refinances each serve a purpose. But knowledge alone does not produce good outcomes. What separates borrowers who benefit from refinancing from those who regret it is not access to options—it is the ability to apply those options within a clear decision framework. This chapter exists to transform understanding into action.

A refinance framework begins with clarity of purpose. Before comparing rates or programs, borrowers must answer a simple question: what problem is this refinance meant to solve? If the answer is vague, the refinance will likely be expensive. Refinancing should either improve cash flow, reduce long-term cost, restructure risk, or support a defined transition. If it does none of these clearly, it is not yet ready to be executed.

The second component of the framework is timeline awareness. Every refinance has a break-even point, whether visible or hidden. Borrowers must understand how long they plan to keep the loan, the home, and the current structure of their finances. FHA refinancing works best when the borrower's timeline allows the benefits to materialize. Short-term ownership paired with long-term refinancing almost always produces disappointment.

Next comes structure alignment. Borrowers should evaluate whether the refinance improves or worsens the shape of their debt. Does it shorten or extend the loan term? Does it preserve or reduce equity? Does it increase predictability or introduce fragility? FHA refinance options are flexible, but flexibility must be directed. Structure determines behavior over time, and behavior determines outcomes.

Risk assessment follows. Every refinance redistributes risk. Lower payments reduce monthly pressure but may increase lifetime cost. Cash-out refinances increase liquidity but reduce margin. Rate-and-term refinances may raise payments but accelerate ownership. Borrowers must decide which risks they are willing to carry and which they are not. There is no risk-free refinance—only trade-offs that must be chosen intentionally.

The fifth element is opportunity cost. Refinancing always closes one door to open another. Money rolled into a loan cannot be invested elsewhere. Equity extracted cannot be used again without consequence. Time added back onto a mortgage cannot be reclaimed. Borrowers who ignore opportunity cost often believe they are gaining something when they are merely exchanging it.

Behavioral honesty is another critical piece of the framework. Refinancing does not change habits. A borrower who uses a refinance to eliminate debt without changing spending patterns is likely to recreate the same pressure later. FHA refinancing is a structural solution. If the problem is behavioral, the refinance will only provide temporary relief.

The framework also demands patience. The best refinance decisions are often preceded by waiting—not for rates, but for readiness. Borrowers who rush because they fear missing out often accept marginal improvements that fail to justify the cost. FHA refinancing rewards preparation more than speed.

Finally, a strong framework includes a forward-looking perspective. Refinancing should support not only today's needs, but tomorrow's options. Borrowers should consider how the refinance affects future refinancing, selling, retirement, or investment plans. FHA loans are part of a longer financial journey, not isolated transactions.

When all these elements come together, refinancing becomes less emotional and more strategic. The borrower is no longer reacting to offers or headlines. They are evaluating decisions against a consistent standard. This is where FHA refinancing becomes empowering rather than confusing.

This book was written to give borrowers that standard. Not to tell them what to do, but to help them decide with confidence. FHA refinance options are tools. The framework determines whether those tools build stability or undermine it.

The final lesson of this book is simple but powerful: the best refinance is not the one with the lowest rate, the biggest check, or the fastest approval. It is the one that aligns with your life, your goals, and your tolerance for risk—both now and in the future. When refinancing is approached this way, it stops being a gamble and becomes a deliberate step forward.

The Refinance That Chose the Borrower

Luis purchased his home with an FHA loan for $350,000 at an interest rate of 4.875 percent. His original loan balance was $337,750, and his monthly principal and interest payment was $1,785. Seven years later, his remaining balance was approximately $288,000. Interest rates had dropped, and Luis received three refinance offers within the same week.

The first was a streamline refinance at 3.75 percent. His payment would drop by $210 per month. Closing costs and mortgage insurance totaling $8,400 would be rolled into the loan, increasing his balance to $296,400. The second was a rate-and-term refinance into a 20-year loan at 3.375 percent. His payment would increase by $160 per month, but total interest savings would exceed $85,000. The third was a cash-out refinance that would allow him to pull $55,000 in equity, increasing his payment by $390 per month.

Luis applied the framework.

He defined his purpose: stability and long-term efficiency, not immediate cash. His timeline was long-term—he planned to stay in the home at least fifteen more years. Structure mattered more than relief. Risk tolerance was moderate. Opportunity cost mattered.

He ran the math.

If he chose the streamline refinance, he would save $210 per month, or $2,520 per year. Over five years, that totaled $12,600—barely exceeding the refinance cost. If he chose the rate-and-term refinance, his payment would increase by $160 per month, or $1,920 per year, but he would save $85,000 in interest over the life of the loan. If he chose the cash-out refinance, he would gain $55,000 now but increase his long-term loan cost by more than $120,000. Luis chose the rate-and-term refinance. The decision was not the most comfortable in the short term, but it aligned with every element of his framework. He traded a modest increase in monthly payment for decades of efficiency and certainty. The refinance did not excite him. It reassured him.

The math did not choose for Luis. The framework did. And because of that, the refinance served him—rather than the other way around.

Chapter 12

After the Refinance — How to Make Sure the Decision Actually Pays Off

Most refinance conversations end the moment the loan funds. The paperwork is signed, the new payment is set, and the borrower moves on. This is where many refinance decisions quietly fail. Refinancing does not succeed because it closes—it succeeds because of what happens afterward. The months and years following a refinance determine whether the decision becomes a financial advantage or a missed opportunity.

A refinance changes structure, but structure alone does not guarantee progress. Lower payments, extended terms, or accessed equity all create new conditions. How the borrower responds to those conditions determines the outcome. FHA refinance programs provide flexibility, but flexibility without follow-through often dissolves into lifestyle creep, complacency, or repeated resets.

One of the most common post-refinance mistakes is treating savings as disposable income. A borrower who lowers their payment by two hundred or three hundred dollars per month may feel immediate relief. Without intention, that relief often gets absorbed into daily spending. Over time, the refinance produces no lasting improvement beyond comfort. The borrower feels better, but their position does not improve.

Another frequent issue is failure to reassess goals after refinancing. A refinance is a reset point. It is an opportunity to redefine priorities, timelines, and strategies. Borrowers who do not revisit their long-term plan often drift. The refinance becomes a pause rather than a pivot. FHA refinancing works best when it marks a transition toward a defined outcome, not simply a reset of obligations.

Mortgage insurance also demands post-refinance awareness. FHA mortgage insurance is not static. Borrowers should understand when it can be removed, how long it will remain, and how refinancing again might affect it. Ignoring mortgage insurance after refinancing often leads to unnecessary costs that could have been avoided with planning.

Debt behavior after refinancing is especially critical for borrowers who used cash-out proceeds or consolidated debt. Eliminating high-interest obligations creates opportunity—but only if the borrower resists replacing them. Reaccumulating consumer debt after a refinance is one of the fastest ways to turn a smart structural decision into a long-term setback. The refinance does not fail immediately. It fails slowly, as habits override structure. Another overlooked aspect of post-refinance success is monitoring break-even points. Borrowers should know when the refinance truly begins to benefit them. This awareness informs future decisions. A borrower who refinances again before reaching break-even often compounds cost instead of benefit. FHA refinancing should be sequenced thoughtfully, not layered impulsively.

Periodic review is essential. Life changes do not stop after refinancing. Income, expenses, and priorities evolve. Borrowers who revisit their mortgage strategy annually maintain control. Those who ignore it for years often miss opportunities or drift into suboptimal positions. FHA loans are long-term instruments, but they still require stewardship.

The emotional aftereffects of refinancing also matter. A refinance can create a false sense of security. Lower payments or access to cash may reduce urgency, leading borrowers to delay saving, investing, or planning. True financial progress requires intentional momentum, not just reduced pressure.

Successful borrowers treat refinancing as a chapter, not a conclusion. The refinance sets the stage. What follows determines whether the decision compounds value or fades into memory. FHA refinance programs give borrowers a second chance to structure their mortgage intelligently. That chance only matters if it is used deliberately.

This chapter exists to remind borrowers that responsibility does not end at closing. In many ways, it begins there. A refinance should simplify life while strengthening the future. That outcome requires awareness, discipline, and periodic adjustment.

Refinancing is not about perfection. It is about progress. Borrowers who stay engaged after refinancing—who track, plan, and adjust—are the ones who extract real value. Those who disengage often wonder years later why the refinance never seemed to change much.

The final truth of FHA refinancing is this: the loan does not decide your future. Your behavior does. Refinancing can support good decisions or mask bad ones. Understanding that distinction is what turns a refinance from a temporary fix into a lasting advantage.

The $275 That Disappeared

Michael refinanced his FHA loan after ten years of ownership. His original loan balance had been $290,000 at a 4.625 percent interest rate. By the time he refinanced, his remaining balance was $238,000. He completed a streamline refinance at 3.5 percent, rolling $7,900 in costs into the new loan. His new balance became $245,900. Michael's monthly principal and interest payment dropped by $275. With escrow unchanged, his total monthly payment reduction felt significant. He told himself the refinance was a success the moment it closed.

For the first few months, Michael enjoyed the breathing room. He dined out more often and upgraded a few subscriptions. The extra $275 disappeared without notice. A year later, he reviewed his finances and realized nothing had changed except his loan balance.

Michael revisited the math. If he had applied the $275 monthly savings toward principal, he would have paid an additional $3,300 per year. Over five years, that would total $16,500—enough to offset much of the refinance cost and shorten his loan meaningfully.

Instead, he had gained comfort but lost momentum.

Michael made a second decision. He redirected the $275 toward principal starting the following month. Over the next four years, he paid an additional $13,200 toward his loan. The refinance finally began to pay off—not because of the loan terms, but because of the behavior that followed.

The refinance did not fail Michael. It waited for him to decide what it would become.

Chapter 13

Future-Proofing Your Mortgage — Making Refinance Decisions You Won't Regret Later

Refinancing always happens in the present, but its consequences live in the future. One of the most overlooked aspects of FHA refinancing is how decisions made today shape options years down the road. Borrowers often evaluate refinances based on current relief or immediate benefit, without considering how the new loan will interact with future goals, market shifts, or life transitions. This chapter exists to extend the borrower's vision beyond the closing table.

A future-proof refinance is one that remains defensible even if circumstances change. Income may rise or fall. Home values may fluctuate. Interest rates may move in either direction. A refinance that only works under ideal conditions is fragile. FHA refinance options are designed to provide flexibility, but flexibility must be preserved intentionally. Every decision either expands or restricts future choices.

Loan term is one of the most significant future-facing variables. Extending a mortgage late into homeownership may improve short-term cash flow, but it can delay financial independence and restrict retirement planning. Conversely, shortening a loan term too aggressively can reduce flexibility during unexpected life events. Future-proofing requires balance—choosing a structure that can absorb disruption without forcing another refinance.

Equity preservation is another core principle. Equity is optionality. It provides the ability to refinance again, sell strategically, relocate, or respond to emergencies. Refinances that aggressively consume equity may feel productive in the moment but often reduce resilience. FHA guidelines intentionally restrict excessive leverage to protect borrowers from overcommitting future resources.

Interest rate decisions also require future awareness. Locking in a low rate feels like a win, but the surrounding structure matters just as much. A low rate paired with high mortgage insurance, excessive costs, or an extended term may underperform a slightly higher rate paired with better structure. Borrowers should evaluate rates within the context of total loan cost and long-term positioning.

Another future-facing consideration is life transition readiness. Career changes, family expansion, downsizing, retirement, and relocation all interact with mortgage structure. A refinance that aligns with today's lifestyle but conflicts with likely transitions creates friction. FHA refinancing works best when it supports adaptability rather than anchoring the borrower to outdated assumptions.

Borrowers should also consider refinancing fatigue. Each refinance carries costs—financial, administrative, and emotional. Frequent refinancing fragments progress and increases the likelihood of diminishing returns. A future-proof refinance aims to reduce the need for additional resets, not invite them.

Tax considerations, while secondary for many borrowers, can also influence long-term outcomes. Changes in deductions, filing status, and income levels alter the real cost of borrowing over time. While FHA refinancing should not be driven by tax speculation, ignoring tax implications entirely can lead to inaccurate projections.

The most resilient refinance decisions are conservative by design. They assume imperfection. They allow room for error. They prioritize sustainability over optimization. FHA programs were created to support stable homeownership, not constant recalibration. Borrowers who adopt this mindset often find that fewer decisions produce better results.

Future-proofing does not mean avoiding refinancing. It means refining the criteria used to approve it. Borrowers who ask,

"Will this decision still make sense if things change?" tend to avoid regret. Those who ask only, "Does this help right now?" often find themselves revisiting the same decision repeatedly.

This chapter encourages borrowers to zoom out. To see refinancing not as a single move, but as part of a longer financial narrative. FHA refinance options can be powerful allies when they are aligned with where a borrower is headed—not just where they stand today.

The goal of future-proofing is not certainty. It is resilience. A refinance that supports resilience continues to serve the borrower even as conditions evolve. That is the standard against which every FHA refinance decision should ultimately be measured.

Planning for the Unknown

Sophia refinanced her FHA loan twelve years after purchasing her home. The original purchase price was $310,000, and her original loan balance was $299,150 at an interest rate of 4.875 percent. By the time she refinanced, her remaining balance was approximately $221,000. Her home appraised for $445,000.

Sophia was offered a streamline refinance that would lower her payment by $230 per month by resetting the loan to a new

30-year term. She was also offered a rate-and-term refinance into a 20-year loan at a slightly higher payment. The streamline refinance felt safer. The rate-and-term refinance felt tighter.

Sophia considered her future. She planned to reduce work hours within ten years. She wanted flexibility, but she also wanted to avoid carrying a mortgage deep into retirement.

She ran the math.

If she chose the streamline refinance, her payment would drop by $230 per month, saving her $2,760 per year. Over ten years, that totaled $27,600. However, the loan would extend well beyond her planned work horizon, and total interest paid over the life of the loan would exceed $160,000.

If she chose the 20-year refinance, her payment would increase by $180 per month. But total interest over the life of the loan would be approximately $82,000—nearly $78,000 less than the streamline option. The loan would be paid off before she turned sixty-five.

Sophia chose the rate-and-term refinance.

Five years later, an unexpected health issue reduced her income. Because she had preserved equity and avoided excessive leverage, she had options. She refinanced again into a modestly longer term with minimal stress. The earlier decision gave her room to adjust.

The refinance aged well—not because it was perfect, but because it anticipated change.

Sophia did not predict the future. She prepared for it. And that preparation turned a single refinance decision into lasting stability.

Chapter 14

Refinancing with Regret in Mind – How Smart Borrowers Avoid the "I Shouldn't Have" Moment

Most refinance mistakes are not obvious at the moment they are made. They surface years later, quietly, when a borrower realizes they are still carrying a mortgage they expected to be done with, or when equity they once had is no longer available. Regret in refinancing rarely comes from doing something reckless. It comes from doing something reasonable without thinking far enough ahead. This chapter is about learning to make refinance decisions that age well—decisions that you will not second-guess five, ten, or twenty years later.

Regret-proof refinancing begins with acknowledging that every refinance has a shadow. The benefit is visible immediately, but the cost often stretches far into the future. Lower payments feel good now. Extended timelines feel invisible until time passes. FHA refinance options are intentionally flexible, which makes them powerful—but flexibility increases the responsibility placed on the borrower to think beyond the present moment.

One of the most common sources of refinance regret is the repeated reset. Borrowers refinance multiple times for incremental improvements, believing each decision stands alone. Over time, these resets accumulate into years of added payments and lost equity growth. No single refinance feels wrong, but the sequence becomes expensive. Regret emerges not from one bad decision, but from a pattern that lacked a stopping point.

Another source of regret is borrowing against stability. Cash-out refinances often feel justified because equity exists. But equity exists precisely because it has not been spent. Borrowers who remove equity without a clear and durable purpose often regret the loss later, especially when life introduces unexpected needs. FHA cash-out refinancing should be evaluated with the assumption that future uncertainty will occur—not with the belief that current conditions will persist.

Regret also forms when borrowers confuse relief with progress. A refinance that reduces stress without improving trajectory can delay real improvement. Borrowers may feel better month to month but realize years later that nothing fundamentally changed. FHA refinancing should ideally reduce stress *and* move the borrower closer to an endpoint—whether that is debt freedom, financial flexibility, or a planned transition.

Loan term regret is particularly common. Borrowers nearing the midpoint of their mortgage often underestimate how fast time passes. Resetting to a new 30-year term at year ten or fifteen may seem harmless, but it can result in payments well into what was expected to be a mortgage-free phase of life. FHA programs allow this because affordability matters—but regret arises when affordability replaces intention.

Borrowers also experience regret when they refinance without preserving options. Equity buffers, manageable payments, and predictable structures create choice. Refinances that eliminate these buffers leave borrowers exposed. FHA refinancing should not remove safety nets unless there is a compelling, irreversible benefit in return.

Another overlooked contributor to regret is emotional timing. Decisions made during fear, urgency, or exhaustion often prioritize immediate comfort over long-term alignment. FHA refinancing can be a stabilizing force during difficult periods, but decisions made under pressure should be conservative by default. Borrowers rarely regret being too cautious during uncertainty. They often regret being too aggressive.

Regret-proofing does not require perfect forecasting. It

requires humility. Borrowers must accept that they do not know exactly what the future will bring. Refinancing should therefore be structured to tolerate change. This means avoiding maximum leverage, minimizing unnecessary resets, and choosing structures that allow adaptation.

The most reliable way to avoid refinance regret is to define an endpoint. Every refinance should answer the question: what does "done" look like? Done with high-interest debt. Done with payment pressure. Done with mortgage payments entirely. Without an endpoint, refinancing becomes an ongoing activity rather than a strategy.

This chapter is not about eliminating risk. It is about choosing risks consciously. FHA refinancing gives borrowers the ability to shift risk across time. Regret occurs when that shift happens unintentionally. Borrowers who refine their decisions through the lens of future reflection tend to make fewer, better refinances.

The ultimate test of a refinance is not whether it felt good at closing. It is whether it still makes sense when circumstances change. Borrowers who keep that test in mind often discover that restraint is as valuable as action. FHA refinancing is a powerful tool—but the most powerful use is often knowing when to stop.

Ten Years Added Back

Eric bought his home with an FHA loan at age thirty-four. The purchase price was $295,000, and his original loan balance was $284,675 at an interest rate of 4.5 percent. His monthly principal and interest payment was $1,443. Fifteen years later, his remaining balance was approximately $178,000. He was on track to have his home paid off before age sixty.

When interest rates dropped, Eric refinanced into a new 30-year FHA loan at 3.625 percent. His payment dropped by $260 per month. Closing costs and mortgage insurance totaling $9,200 were rolled into the loan, increasing his balance to $187,200. The refinance felt like a win.

Eric used the savings for lifestyle upgrades. The lower payment blended into daily life. Five years passed.

At age fifty-four, Eric reviewed his mortgage and realized he now had twenty-five years remaining instead of ten. The refinance had added fifteen years back onto his loan. He ran the math.

Before refinancing, his remaining interest over fifteen years would have been approximately $52,000. After refinancing, total interest over thirty years would exceed $128,000. The refinance had added roughly $76,000 in interest cost.

Eric refinanced again—this time into a 15-year loan. The payment increased significantly, forcing lifestyle adjustments he hadn't planned for. The correction was possible, but it came with stress.

The original refinance was not reckless. It was reasonable. But it lacked an endpoint. Eric did not regret refinancing. He regretted refinancing without thinking about who he wanted to be ten years later.

The math didn't punish him immediately. It waited. And by the time it spoke clearly, the decision had already aged.

Chapter 15

The Last Refinance You'll Ever Need – Designing an Exit, Not a Loop

Most borrowers think of refinancing as a recurring option. A tool that can be used again and again whenever rates shift or life changes. While FHA refinance programs do allow flexibility, the most successful homeowners approach refinancing with a different mindset. They do not ask, "How can I refinance again later?" They ask, "How do I structure this so I don't need to?" This chapter is about designing an exit strategy—not from homeownership, but from unnecessary refinancing.

A refinance loop occurs when borrowers repeatedly reset their loan without advancing toward a defined outcome. Each refinance feels helpful on its own, but collectively they extend timelines, dilute equity growth, and create dependency on future refinancing to maintain comfort. FHA programs were never intended to support perpetual resets. They were designed to stabilize borrowers until they could move forward deliberately.

The concept of a "final refinance" does not mean the borrower will never refinance again under any circumstance. It means structuring the loan in a way that aligns so well with long-term goals that future refinancing becomes optional rather than necessary. This requires clarity, restraint, and a willingness to trade short-term convenience for long-term control.

Designing a final refinance begins with defining the desired endpoint. For some borrowers, the endpoint is a paid-off home by retirement. For others, it is a fixed, predictable payment that fits permanently within their budget. For some, it is a loan structure that supports semi-retirement, business ownership, or geographic flexibility. Refinancing without defining this endpoint almost guarantees repetition.

Loan term is central to this decision. Extending a mortgage late into homeownership may reduce payments today but often creates regret later. Conversely, choosing a shorter term too aggressively can strain cash flow and force future adjustments. The final refinance balances ambition with sustainability. It should feel firm, not fragile.

Equity strategy also plays a decisive role. A final refinance preserves optionality. It avoids maximum leverage. It leaves room for unexpected needs without forcing another reset. Borrowers who extract equity late in the journey often discover they have traded flexibility for temporary comfort. FHA refinancing rewards those who stop extracting and start consolidating progress. Another hallmark of a final refinance is payment realism. The payment should be affordable not just today, but under less favorable conditions. Income disruptions, inflation, healthcare costs, and lifestyle changes must be considered. A refinance that only works under ideal circumstances invites future stress.

Behavioral alignment matters just as much as math. Borrowers who rely on refinancing to manage spending are unlikely to reach a final refinance naturally. The final refinance requires that financial habits support the structure—not fight it. Without this alignment, even the best-designed loan will eventually be challenged.

Timing the final refinance is less about interest rates and more about readiness. It often occurs when income stabilizes, priorities clarify, and the borrower shifts from growth mode to preservation mode. This timing looks different for everyone. FHA refinance programs accommodate many paths, but the borrower must choose when to stop optimizing and start settling in.

The final refinance also requires emotional maturity. It means accepting that the "best possible rate" may not be necessary. That chasing perfection can undermine progress. That a good, durable decision often outperforms a theoretically optimal one that demands constant adjustment. This chapter challenges borrowers to think of refinancing as a means to an end, not an ongoing tactic. FHA refinancing should simplify life over time, not complicate it. The goal is not to win the refinance game—it is to exit it with dignity, stability, and control.

When borrowers design a refinance with an endpoint in mind, something changes. Decisions slow down. Trade-offs become clearer. Urgency fades. Refinancing becomes deliberate rather than reactive. That shift is the difference between borrowing as a habit and borrowing as a strategy.

The last refinance you'll ever need is not defined by the market. It is defined by alignment. When the loan matches your life so well that future refinancing feels unnecessary, you have reached the true objective of FHA refinancing.

The Refinance That Closed the Door

Patricia purchased her home with an FHA loan at age thirty-eight. The purchase price was $360,000, and her original loan balance was $347,400 at an interest rate of 4.75 percent. Her monthly principal and interest payment was $1,812. Fifteen years later, her remaining loan balance was approximately $214,000. She had refinanced twice already, each time lowering her payment but extending her timeline. At age fifty-three, Patricia reviewed her mortgage and realized she still had twenty-three years remaining. Retirement was no longer abstract. She wanted certainty.

She was offered another streamline refinance that would lower her payment by $190 per month by resetting to a new 30-year term. She was also offered a rate-and-term refinance into a 15-year FHA loan at 3.375 percent. The payment would increase by $310 per month.

Patricia ran the math.

If she chose the streamline refinance, her monthly savings would total $2,280 per year. Over ten years, that would be $22,800. But the loan would stretch into her late seventies, and total interest paid would exceed $110,000.

If she chose the 15-year refinance, her payment would increase by $310 per month, or $3,720 per year. But total interest over the life of the loan would be approximately $52,000—saving nearly $58,000. The home would be paid off before she turned sixty-eight.

Patricia adjusted her budget. She reduced discretionary spending and redirected one bonus per year toward reserves. The payment increase felt firm but manageable. Five years later, Patricia experienced a job transition. Because she had preserved equity and avoided further resets, she had options.

The refinance did not trap her—it supported her.

Patricia didn't choose the refinance that felt easiest. She chose the one that let her be done.

The math did not demand perfection. It demanded commitment. And in return, it gave her something far more valuable than savings—finality.

Chapter 16

Beyond the Mortgage — How Refinancing Shapes Freedom, Legacy, and Choice

Most borrowers think of a mortgage as a payment. More thoughtful borrowers think of it as a liability to be managed. The most strategic borrowers, however, understand that a mortgage is also a lever—one that influences freedom, stress, opportunity, and legacy. Refinancing decisions, especially within the FHA system, do not just affect monthly budgets. They quietly shape how much flexibility a borrower has later in life, how resilient a household becomes during uncertainty, and what options exist for the next generation.

Refinancing becomes most dangerous when it is viewed narrowly. A refinance is never just a rate change or a payment adjustment. It is a redesign of obligation across time. FHA refinance programs allow borrowers to move obligations forward, backward, or sideways in ways that feel subtle at first but become significant over decades. This chapter invites borrowers to zoom out—to consider not just affordability, but autonomy. Financial freedom is not defined by income alone. It is defined by control over fixed obligations. A borrower with a modest income and a predictable, diminishing mortgage often has more freedom than a high earner locked into perpetual resets. FHA refinancing can either accelerate freedom or delay it indefinitely, depending on whether the borrower uses it to reduce dependency or reinforce it.

One of the most overlooked impacts of refinancing is how it affects decision-making power later in life. A borrower entering their fifties with a shrinking mortgage has options: career changes, reduced work hours, geographic mobility, or entrepreneurship. A borrower with a reset 30-year loan at the same age may feel financially boxed in, even if their payment is low. FHA refinancing can quietly decide which of these futures becomes available.

Legacy is another dimension rarely considered. A home with low or no debt is not just an asset—it is stability that can be passed on, leveraged responsibly, or preserved during family transitions. Repeated refinancing that strips equity or extends timelines often converts a generational asset into a perpetual obligation. FHA loans were designed to promote ownership stability, but refinancing must be used carefully to preserve that intention.

Borrowers also underestimate how refinancing affects risk exposure over time. Debt that persists longer increases exposure to market cycles, health events, employment disruptions, and policy changes. Refinancing that shortens timelines reduces exposure. Refinancing that extends timelines increases it. FHA refinancing should ideally move borrowers toward less vulnerability, not more.

Another important consideration is psychological freedom. Carrying long-term debt affects how people experience work, stress, and opportunity. Borrowers who know their mortgage has an endpoint often make bolder, healthier decisions. Those who feel trapped by extended timelines often default to caution—not because they lack ambition, but because their obligations limit tolerance for risk. Refinancing decisions contribute directly to this internal dynamic.

This chapter does not argue that every borrower should aggressively pay off their mortgage. It argues that every borrower should *choose* their relationship with debt intentionally. FHA refinancing provides tools to redesign that relationship, but it cannot define values. Borrowers must decide what they want their money to do for them over time.

Refinancing also interacts with intergenerational planning. A mortgage that is nearly gone can support aging parents, adult children, or unexpected responsibilities without panic. A heavily leveraged home limits that capacity. FHA refinancing should be evaluated not just through personal benefit, but through family resilience.

The final stage of mortgage strategy is not optimization—it is simplification. Reducing complexity, reducing resets, and reducing dependency on future refinancing create peace of mind that no interest rate can match. FHA refinancing can either simplify life or entangle it further. The difference lies in intention.

This chapter encourages borrowers to stop asking, "Can I refinance?" and start asking, "What kind of future does this refinance support?" When refinancing decisions are filtered through that question, many tempting offers lose their appeal. Others gain clarity and purpose.

Beyond the mortgage lies choice. Choice over time, work, location, and legacy. Refinancing is one of the few tools borrowers have to shape that landscape deliberately. Used wisely, it can compress decades of stress into years of effort. Used casually, it can stretch years of effort into decades of obligation.

The true success of FHA refinancing is not measured at closing. It is measured years later, when borrowers realize they have options—and the freedom to use them.

Buying Back the Next 20 Years

Daniel bought his home with an FHA loan at age thirty-six. The purchase price was $340,000, and his original loan balance was $328,100 at an interest rate of 4.875 percent. His monthly principal and interest payment was $1,736. Over time, Daniel's income grew, but he refinanced twice to lower payments and free cash flow.

At age fifty, Daniel reviewed his mortgage and realized he still owed $262,000 with twenty-eight years remaining. The payment was comfortable, but the timeline was not. He wanted the option to step away from full-time work by sixty.

Daniel evaluated two options. A streamline refinance would reduce his payment by $210 per month by resetting the loan again. A rate-and-term refinance into a 15-year FHA loan at 3.5 percent would increase his payment by $420 per month.

Daniel ran the math.

If he chose the streamline refinance, he would save $2,520 per year. Over ten years, that would total $25,200. However, total interest paid over the life of the loan would exceed $145,000, and the mortgage would follow him into his seventies.

If he chose the 15-year refinance, the higher payment would cost an additional $5,040 per year. Over fifteen years, that totaled $75,600. But total interest paid would be approximately $68,000—saving more than $77,000—and the mortgage would be gone by age sixty-five.

Daniel restructured his spending and committed half of his annual bonuses to reserves. The payment increase felt deliberate, not punitive.

At age sixty, Daniel reduced his work hours. At sixty-five, his mortgage was gone. The refinance did not maximize comfort in the moment—it maximized choice later.

Daniel didn't eliminate his mortgage to feel wealthy. He eliminated it to feel free.

The refinance did not follow him into the next chapter of life. And that was the point.

Final Thoughts

Refinancing with Clarity, Confidence, and Control

If there is one truth that should remain with you after finishing this book, it is this: refinancing is not a transaction—it is a decision that reshapes time. Every FHA refinance option discussed in these chapters exists to move financial weight forward, backward, or sideways across your life. The power of that movement is not found in rates, programs, or lender promises. It is found in your understanding of what you are trading, what you are gaining, and what you are choosing to carry into the future.

Many borrowers approach refinancing believing they are making a small adjustment. A few hundred dollars per month. A slightly lower rate. A reset that feels harmless. But mortgages are not small instruments. They are long commitments that quietly define flexibility, stress, and opportunity. FHA refinancing magnifies this effect because it is designed to be accessible. Accessibility is a gift—but only when paired with intention.

Throughout this book, you have seen that FHA refinance options are not interchangeable. Streamline refinances prioritize simplicity and relief. Rate-and-term refinances prioritize structure and efficiency. Cash-out refinances prioritize liquidity and leverage. None of these paths are inherently good or bad. They are context-dependent. The mistake is not choosing the "wrong" option. The mistake is choosing without alignment.

Alignment means your refinance supports your life as it actually is—not as it was when you bought the home, and not as lenders assume it should be. Alignment means your loan structure reflects your income stability, your tolerance for risk, your family obligations, and your long-term plans. When refinancing lacks alignment, it often creates the illusion of progress while quietly delaying real outcomes.

One of the most important lessons in this book is that relief is not the same as improvement. A refinance that reduces pressure without changing direction can be useful—but it should not be confused with a strategy. Relief buys time. Strategy determines what you do with that time. FHA refinancing works best when it provides both: breathing room *and* momentum.

Another critical takeaway is that refinancing is cumulative. One refinance rarely defines a borrower's outcome. Sequences do. A single reset may be harmless. Repeated resets without an endpoint often become expensive. Many borrowers do not regret refinancing—they regret refinancing *again*, without realizing they were drifting into a loop. Awareness breaks that cycle.

You have also seen that equity is not a reward—it is responsibility. Equity represents deferred consumption. It exists because you did not spend it earlier. FHA cash-out refinancing allows you to convert that stored value into present flexibility, but the conversion is never free. Borrowers who treat equity casually often discover too late that they have traded future options for short-term comfort. Borrowers who treat equity deliberately often unlock stability that lasts decades.

Timing, too, has emerged as more personal than market-driven. Interest rates matter, but life timing matters more. A refinance executed at the right moment in your life can outperform a technically better refinance done at the wrong time. Waiting for perfection often costs more than acting with clarity. FHA refinancing rewards readiness, not prediction.

Perhaps the most important shift this book encourages is a change in mindset. Instead of asking, "Can I refinance?" the more powerful question becomes, "What does this refinance make easier—and what does it make harder—five, ten, or twenty years from now?" That question reframes the decision from short-term optimization to long-term stewardship. Refinancing should not increase dependence on future refinancing. Ideally, it should reduce it. Each well-designed refinance simplifies your financial life rather than complicating it. It should narrow your range of stress, not widen it. It should move you closer to an endpoint you recognize and value.

That endpoint will differ for every borrower. For some, it is a paid-off home before retirement. For others, it is a permanently manageable payment that allows flexibility in work and lifestyle. For some, it is the ability to use their home as a stable base while building wealth elsewhere. The correct endpoint is not universal—but the need to define one is.

This book was written to give you tools, not instructions. FHA refinancing does not require perfection. It requires honesty. Honesty about your habits. Honesty about your risk tolerance. Honesty about your future self. Borrowers who approach refinancing with humility tend to make fewer, better decisions. Borrowers who chase certainty often end up repeating the same decision under different conditions.

If there is a single discipline that separates borrowers who benefit from refinancing from those who regret it, it is restraint. Knowing when *not* to refinance is just as powerful as knowing how. FHA programs make refinancing accessible, but accessibility should not be mistaken for obligation. You do not need to act just because an option exists.

As you move forward, remember that refinancing is not a verdict on past decisions. It is an opportunity to redesign your path from this point onward. Every borrower arrives at this moment with a different history. FHA refinancing does not judge that history. It gives you the chance to respond to it intelligently.

The goal of this book has never been to persuade you to refinance. It has been to equip you to decide. To slow the decision down. To replace urgency with clarity. To replace noise with math. To replace fear with structure.

When refinancing is done with clarity, confidence follows. When confidence replaces doubt, control returns. And when you regain control over your largest financial obligation, everything else becomes easier to manage.

That is the true promise of FHA refinancing—not cheaper payments, not faster approvals, not flexible rules—but the ability to shape your financial life deliberately rather than reactively.

Carry that mindset forward. Let refinancing serve you once, well, and with purpose. And when you look back years from now, let this be the moment you chose understanding over impulse—and strategy over repetition.

The FHA Homeownership & Wealth Series

Complete Roadmap: From First-Time Buyer to Long-Term Wealth Builder

The FHA Homeownership & Wealth Series is designed as a progressive journey. Each book builds on the previous one, guiding borrowers from basic understanding to confident ownership, strategic financing, and long-term wealth creation. Readers can enter at any stage, but those who follow the full roadmap gain the clearest, fastest path to results.

This series is structured to meet borrowers exactly where they are—and show them what comes next.

Phase 1: Foundation & Confidence (Books 1–3)

Understanding FHA and realizing you qualify

These books eliminate confusion, fear, and misinformation. They are designed to answer the most important early question: *Is homeownership actually possible for me?*

Book 1 – FHA Loans Explained for Beginners How FHA Mortgages Work, Who Qualifies, and Why They're One of the Easiest Paths to Homeownership This is the foundation of the entire series. Readers learn how FHA loans work, why they exist, and how to evaluate FHA realistically using math instead of myths. This book builds confidence and replaces hesitation with clarity.

Book 2 – Buying Your First Home with FHA A Step-by-Step Guide to Purchasing a Home with Low Down Payment and Flexible Credit Rules This book turns understanding into action. Readers learn the full buying process—from pre-approval to closing—so they know exactly what to expect and how to avoid common first-time buyer mistakes.

Book 3 – FHA Loans for Borrowers with Low Credit or Past Credit Issues How to Get Approved with FHA Even with Late Payments, Collections, or a Low Credit Score This book is for borrowers who believe their credit disqualifies them. It explains FHA's second-chance philosophy and shows how recovery, not perfection, determines approval.

Phase 2: Income Reality & Property Flexibility (Books 4–6)

Qualifying with real-life finances and real homes

These books expand what readers believe is possible by addressing income types, property types, and cash requirements.

Book 4 – FHA Loans for Self-Employed, 1099 & Gig Workers How Business Owners and Independent Contractors Qualify for FHA Home Loans This book demystifies income calculations for non-traditional earners and shows how FHA accommodates modern work patterns.

Book 5 – FHA Loans for Fixer-Uppers, Condos & Non-Perfect Homes How to Buy Homes That Need Repairs or Don't Fit Traditional Loan Guidelines Readers learn how FHA views property condition and how renovation and condo options expand buying opportunities.

Book 6 – FHA Loan Limits, Down Payment & Closing Costs How Much You Can Borrow and How to Bring Less Money to the Closing Table This book focuses on numbers. Readers learn how FHA loan limits work, how to reduce cash to close, and how seller credits and assistance programs change affordability.

Phase 3: Optimization & Refinancing Strategy (Books 7–8)

Using FHA beyond the purchase

These books show how FHA loans evolve with the borrower.

Book 7 – FHA Refinance Options Made Simple Streamline, Rate-and-Term, and Cash-Out Refinancing Explained for Homeowners Readers learn how FHA supports refinancing, payment reduction, and financial repositioning over time.

Book 8 – Using an FHA Cash-Out Refinance to Build Wealth How to Turn Home Equity into Cash Without Selling Your Home This book introduces equity as a strategic tool, not just a number on paper, while emphasizing responsible use.

Phase 4: Income & Expansion (Books 9–10)

Turning ownership into leverage

These books shift the reader from homeowner to strategist.

Book 9 – Buying Multi-Unit Homes with FHA How to Purchase 2–4 Unit Properties, Live in One, and Rent the Rest Readers learn how FHA enables owner-occupied investing and rent-offset strategies that dramatically reduce housing costs.

Book 10 – FHA Loan Myths, Mistakes & Borrower Strategies What Most Buyers Get Wrong—and How Smart Borrowers Win with FHA Loans This is the strategic wrap-up book that reinforces best practices, avoids costly errors, and helps readers think like informed borrowers.

About the Author

Joe Correa is a mortgage professional, educator, and financial strategist dedicated to helping everyday people understand homeownership, credit, and wealth-building without confusion or intimidation. With years of hands-on experience in the mortgage industry, Joe has worked with first-time buyers, self-employed borrowers, credit-challenged families, and aspiring investors who were often told "no" before learning what was actually possible.

What sets Joe apart is his ability to translate complex lending rules into clear, practical guidance. Rather than relying on theory, his work is grounded in real-world scenarios, real numbers, and real borrower outcomes. He believes that most people do not fail to buy homes because they lack income or discipline, but because they lack accurate information. His mission is to replace myths with math and fear with understanding.

Joe specializes in FHA loans because he has seen firsthand how transformative they can be when used correctly. He views FHA not as a last resort, but as one of the most powerful entry points into homeownership and long-term wealth—especially for borrowers navigating modern financial realities such as student loans, variable income, credit recovery, or limited savings. Through his writing, Joe teaches borrowers how to think strategically, act confidently, and use lending tools intentionally rather than emotionally.

In addition to his mortgage work, Joe is the creator of multiple educational programs and book series focused on homeownership, credit building, refinancing strategies, and financial independence. His approach emphasizes sustainability over speculation and progress over perfection. He is known for breaking down decisions into simple frameworks that empower readers to make smart choices at every stage of their journey.

Joe's writing style reflects his core belief: financial education should be accessible, practical, and empowering. He does not promise shortcuts or hype outcomes. Instead, he provides clarity, structure, and realistic paths forward—so readers can move from uncertainty to ownership with confidence.

When he is not writing or working with borrowers, Joe continues developing educational resources designed to help families build stability, equity, and long-term opportunity through informed financial decisions.

How to Get a Personalized FHA Review

If you found this book helpful, you may want to see how FHA loan options apply to your specific income, credit profile, cash to close, and homeownership goals.

Every borrower's situation is different. FHA guidelines, loan limits, interest rates, mortgage insurance, and available options vary based on income type, credit history, debt levels, savings, property type, and state guidelines. The examples in this book are educational, but your personal FHA eligibility, payment range, and strategy can only be determined through an individualized review.

As a licensed mortgage broker, I offer a **Personalized FHA Review** designed to show you: • Whether you currently qualify for an FHA loan • Your realistic home price and monthly payment range • How much cash you may need for down payment and closing costs • How credit, debt, or income factors affect your approval • Whether FHA is the best option for you now or later • What steps, if any, would strengthen your position

This review is fast, confidential, and focused entirely on helping you make informed homeownership decisions—without pressure or obligation.

To request your personalized FHA review, visit:https://finibimortgage.carrd.co/

You may also submit your information through the QR code provided in this book.

Your financial profile already tells a story.This review shows you how FHA lenders will read it.

Yours truly,

Joseph G. Correa

Licensed Mortgage Broker, Finibi Mortgage

Educational & Financial Disclaimer

This book is provided for educational and informational purposes only. The content is intended to help readers better understand FHA loans, homeownership concepts, and general mortgage strategies, but it does not constitute financial advice, legal advice, tax advice, or lending approval. Mortgage guidelines, FHA requirements, interest rates, loan programs, and qualification standards are subject to change and may vary based on individual circumstances, lender overlays, geographic location, and market conditions.

Nothing in this book should be interpreted as a guarantee of loan approval, loan terms, interest rates, or eligibility. All examples, scenarios, calculations, and illustrations are for educational purposes only and are not intended to represent actual loan offers or outcomes. Individual results will vary based on credit profile, income stability, debt obligations, assets, property characteristics, and lender-specific requirements.

Readers are encouraged to consult with a licensed mortgage professional, financial advisor, tax professional, or legal advisor before making any financial or real estate decisions. This book does not replace personalized advice or professional review. Any decisions made based on the information in this book are the sole responsibility of the reader.

The author and publisher are not responsible for any actions taken by readers as a result of the information provided in this book. While every effort has been made to ensure accuracy at the time of publication, no representation or warranty is made regarding the completeness, reliability, or current applicability of the information contained herein.

By reading this book, you acknowledge that homeownership and mortgage decisions involve risk and personal responsibility, and you agree that the author and publisher are not liable for any financial outcomes, losses, or damages that may result from reliance on this material.

This book is designed to educate, not to instruct or advise on individual financial decisions. Its purpose is to provide general understanding so readers can ask better questions, seek appropriate professional guidance, and make informed choices based on their unique circumstances.

Risk Disclosure

Homeownership and mortgage financing involve financial risk. While FHA loans are designed to increase access to homeownership and provide flexible qualification standards, they do not eliminate risk, and outcomes may vary based on individual circumstances, market conditions, and personal financial decisions. Purchasing or refinancing a home requires a long-term financial commitment and should be evaluated carefully.

Housing markets can fluctuate. Property values may increase or decrease over time, and there is no guarantee that a home will appreciate in value. Economic conditions, interest rate changes, local market factors, and unforeseen events can affect property values, mortgage payments, and resale opportunities. Borrowers should be prepared for the possibility that home values may remain flat or decline during certain periods.

Mortgage payments represent a fixed obligation that must be met regardless of changes in income, employment status, health, or personal circumstances. Failure to make mortgage payments may result in late fees, credit damage, default, or foreclosure. Borrowers should ensure they have adequate income stability, savings, and contingency planning before entering into any mortgage obligation.

FHA loans include mortgage insurance, which increases the total cost of borrowing. While mortgage insurance enables access to lower down payments and more flexible credit standards, it may remain in place for a significant portion of the loan term unless refinanced or otherwise removed under applicable guidelines. Borrowers should understand how mortgage insurance affects monthly payments and long-term costs.

Refinancing, selling, or leveraging home equity is not guaranteed to be available in the future. These options depend on market conditions, interest rates, credit profile, equity levels, and lender requirements at the time of action. Borrowers should not assume future refinancing opportunities or equity access when making initial homeownership decisions.

Rental income, including income from multi-unit properties or converted rentals, is not guaranteed. Vacancies, maintenance costs, market conditions, tenant behavior, and regulatory changes can impact rental cash flow. Borrowers considering rental strategies should evaluate these risks carefully and avoid relying on projected rental income for financial stability.

This book does not provide investment advice or predict financial outcomes. All examples and scenarios are illustrative only and should not be relied upon as forecasts or guarantees. Readers are responsible for conducting their own due diligence and seeking professional advice when appropriate.

By choosing to pursue homeownership or mortgage financing, readers acknowledge the presence of risk and accept responsibility for their financial decisions. The author and publisher are not responsible for any losses, damages, or adverse outcomes resulting from actions taken based on the information provided in this book.

This disclosure is intended to promote informed decision-making, not discourage homeownership. Understanding risk is a critical part of using FHA loans responsibly and sustainably.

www.ingramcontent.com/pod-product-compliance
Lightning Source LLC
LaVergne TN
LVHW022231200926
848481LV00006B/2216